P9-CBM-439

HOW TO BE YOUR OWN
ARCHITECT

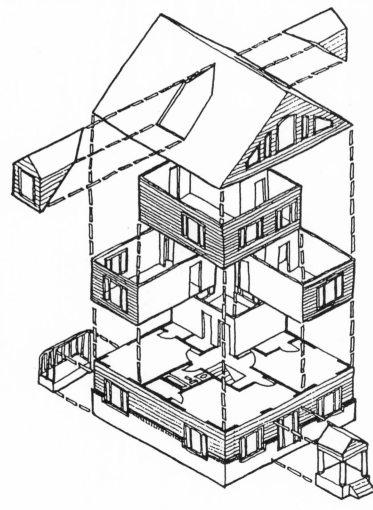

A RESIDENTIAL DESIGN HANDBOOK

SCOTT T. BALLARD/AIA

Betterway Publications, Inc.

728.37
BAL

Published by Betterway Publications, Inc.
White Hall, Virginia, 22987

Cover Design by Josef Beery

Copyright © 1987 by Scott Ballard, AIA

All rights reserved. No part of this book may be reproduced by any means, except by a reviewer who wishes to quote brief excerpts in connection with a review in a newspaper or magazine, without permission of the publisher.

Library of Congress Cataloging-in-Publication Data

Ballard, Scott T. 1947-
    How To Be Your Own Architect

    Bibliography : p.
    Includes index
    1. Architecture, Domestic--Amateurs' Manuals.
2. Architecture, Domestic--Designs and Plans.
I. Title.
NA7115. B29 1987 728.3'7 87-6338
ISBN 0-932620-72-8

Printed in the United States of America
0   9   8   7   6   5   4   3   2   1

Dedicated to my beautiful wife, Carolyn Rose,
without whose distracting presence this book
might have been finished sooner.

TABLE OF CONTENTS

TABLE OF CONTENTS

"Living well is the best revenge."

This book was written for those people who already know what they want in a house and would like a little professional help to bring it all together. It was also written for those people who think it might be fun to design their own house if they knew where to start and where to go from there.

The basic design processes are explained through the use of an example in a step-by-step method. Typical problems are identified and solutions are presented, evaluated, and refined in a concise and logical manner using the professional techniques of the architect. We will cover everything from the basic tools required to begin work through the financial principles involved. The book describes in simple form how you can design a home, keep it in an established budget, and make your dream into a reality. But this is only the beginning of good design.

The premise of this book is to go beyond the mere one-two-three exercise in home design. I want to introduce the reader to the basic architectural principles - order and form, massing and composition, etc. - to challenge the reader to create on a more sophisticated level and to make available the concepts which can bring meaning to steel and stone. These concepts are explained in plain language and are illustrated by examples taken from some of the highlights of the history of architecture.

Designing your own home can be an enriching experience. You will be forced to intensely study your own lifestyle and preferences. It places you, as the designer, in a position of awareness of your physical environment in terms of the natural elements and man-made shelter. It allows you to create a personal habitat which will enhance your living experiences on a daily basis. Finally, if done well, it will provide you with a more thoughtful and meaningful existence.

Good Luck

Scott Ballard, AIA

TOOLS

Just as a poor workman may not be allowed to blame his tools for his lack of craftsmanship, he will not get very far without them. There are some few basic implements which will be necessary if one is to go beyond the sketch phase in house design but they are few and inexpensive. The following pages list the basic items along with their function and approximate price. In most cases several alternatives are presented for the same task, differing only in convenience and price. A professional set-up can be had for around $100.00 total but a good starter kit can be as low as $25.00.

TOOLS

THE IDEAL WORKSTATION

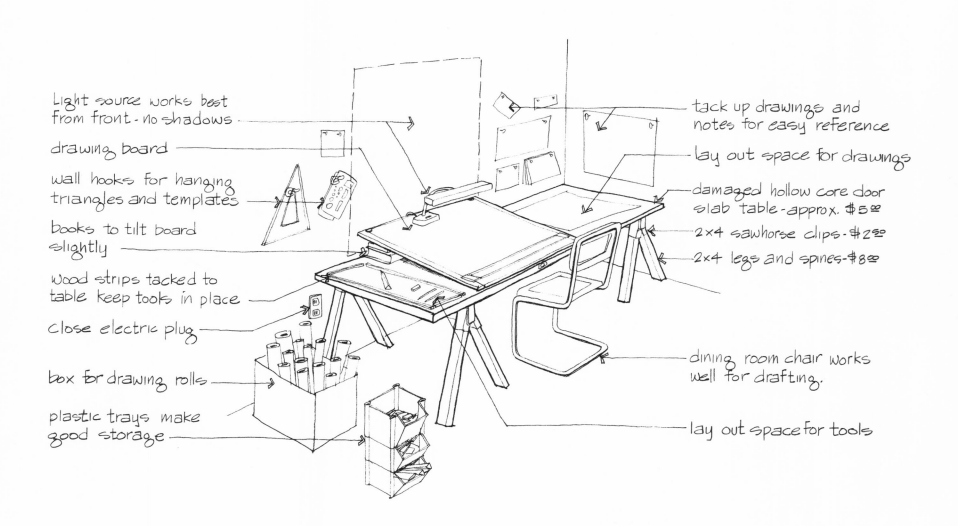

Light source works best from front - no shadows

drawing board

wall hooks for hanging triangles and templates

books to tilt board slightly

wood strips tacked to table keep tools in place

close electric plug

box for drawing rolls

plastic trays make good storage

tack up drawings and notes for easy reference

lay out space for drawings

damaged hollow core door slab table - approx. $5⁰⁰

2×4 sawhorse clips - $2⁰⁰

2×4 legs and spines - $8⁰⁰

dining room chair works well for drafting.

lay out space for tools

It is true that some great building design concepts are created with only a pen and a napkin. Nevertheless, for a beginner there are a few basic drawing tools which can be of assistance in the design process. All are available at any local art supply store.

TRACING PAPER

Very thin and inexpensive paper bought in rolls and used for overlay sketching. Instead of erasing, a new layer is placed over the old sketch for refining the design. This process gives the freedom of a blank page but the guidance of the form below. Layer upon layer of sketches are used and discarded as a design evolves. Buy a 12" roll for $4.00.

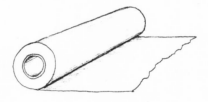

SCALES

A plastic or wooden 'ruler' with scaled down increments of feet and inches used to accurately measure at a much reduced size. Architects scale ranges from 1"=16' to 1"=4', used for building dimensions. Engineers scale range from 1"=60' to 1"=10', used for site dimensions. Buy both for $3.50 each.

TOOLS

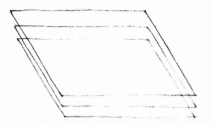

VELLUM DRAWING PAPER:

A very strong translucent paper which one can copy through, but strong enough to be erased many times without damage. This paper is for final drawings. 18" x 24" should be an adequate size sheet for most plans. About 75¢ per sheet.

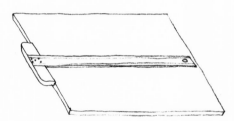

T-SQUARE

A straight edge with a perpendicular end piece which rides against the edge of the drawing board allowing one to draw parallel lines easily. Priced around $20.00.

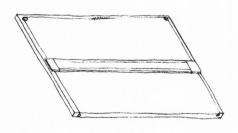

PARALLEL BAR

A straight edge usually rigged with cables and pullies which keep the bar parallel as it moves up and down the board. A 42" long bar costs about $55.00.

TRIANGLES

Clear plexiglass instruments used with a parallel bar to draw parallel lines perpendicular to or at some angle to the bar.

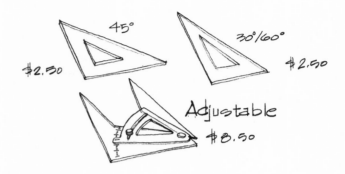

DRAWING BOARD

A wooden slab usually with a vinyl cover and metal edges used as a drawing surface. Some newer models can be purchased quite reasonably with a parallel bar already attached for about $45.00. Minimum size for our purposes is about 21" x 26". This can be placed on an ordinary table top for a good work arrangement.

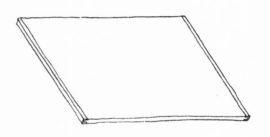

PENCILS

Any pencil will do. Architects use mechanical lead holders in order to use different hardness leads for different tasks. This type requires a special sharpener. Whatever type pencil you select, use a fairly hard lead (H or 2H) so it will stay sharp longer and smudge less.

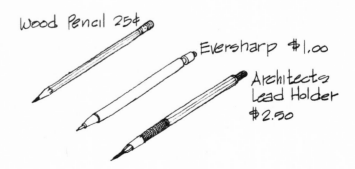

Wood Pencil 25¢

Eversharp $1.00

Architects Lead Holder $2.50

TOOLS

ERASERS

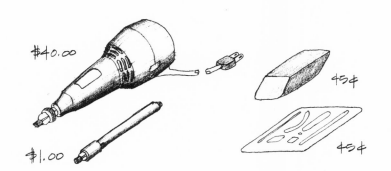

$40.00

$1.00

45¢

45¢

Any eraser will do. Architects use an electric eraser which allows them to erase a small portion of a drawing without spreading the destruction too far. The same thing can be accomplished with a manual eraser and an eraser shield.

DRAFTING TAPE

$1.25

Similar to masking tape, used to hold the drawing in place on the board.

EXACTO KNIFE

A metal knife handle which holds razor sharp steel blades used for cutting paper, cardboard, model building, etc. Don't forget extra blades. Be careful. Cost $1.29

TEMPLATES

A thin plastic sheet with shapes cut out for easy reproduction of that shape. Buy a general residential template with circles, squares, restroom and kitchen fixtures at ¼" and ⅛" scales. About $2.50.

PENCIL SHARPENERS

Many types of pencil sharpeners are available, manual and electric, in a wide range of prices. Make sure your sharpener works for your pencil.

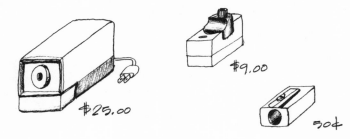

$25.00

$9.00

50¢

PARALLEL GLIDER

This is a small parallel bar that rolls on grooved wheels which really do keep it parallel. It even has a compass engraved into its top so it may be placed at an exact angle to another line and maintain that angle. It could be substituted for a parallel bar for smaller drawings. Costs about $10.00.

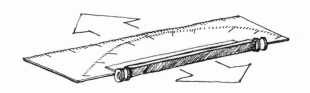

TOOLS

SCRAPBOOK

A scrapbook can be the easiest way to visualize the types of spaces, materials, details, etc. you want in your home, and the best way to convey the idea to someone else. It is a good idea to collect photographs, plans, etc. from newspapers and magazines or sketch ideas as they come to you, and organize them in a scrapbook for the time you actually begin to design. This can speed up the design process considerably and make you more confident that you are designing what you want.

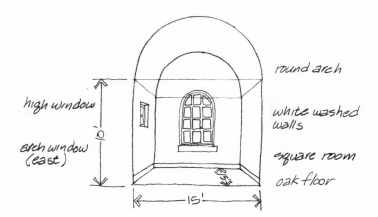

high window

arch window (east)

round arch

white washed walls

square room

oak floor

15'

LEARN TO LOOK

Also, when you are inside a space that feels good, try to analyze what it is about the space that contributes to that good feeling. Note the approximate width, length, height, shape, window and door locations, color, etc. and record them in your scrapbook. In this way you will begin to really see the spaces around you instead of just feeling them.

SITE

The most outstanding feature of real estate is that each piece is unique unto itself, usually for many reasons but at least in its location. This notion is very important to site design because it reminds us that there will be a planning solution for each site that will be superior to any other. Before we begin to plan the structure it will be necessary to do an in-depth analysis of the site itself. The study will include physical features (trees, topography, orientation, access, drainage, neighboring structures, etc.), legal characteristics (building set-back lines, height limitations, zoning, easements, etc.), and psychological aspects (views, noise sources, neighboring activity areas, sun-rise and sun-set, etc.). As we examine and chart these items we are slowly gaining an understanding of the special demands of the site and this knowledge helps us in the planning of the proper house for that particular site. The following pages explain how this is done.

Of course we can design a house for a typical urban lot with a great deal of success because lot sizes are fairly uniform. This has been done in the TRANSFORMER chapter, pp. 91, by selecting a minimum lot size with which to work. The resulting general plan can later be modified to take better advantage of a particular site.

SITE

Each lot is represented on a plot plan by a scale drawing with surveyor's metes and bounds. The metes and bounds record the compass angle of a boundary and its length. Also shown are the building line and any easements, which cannot be violated.

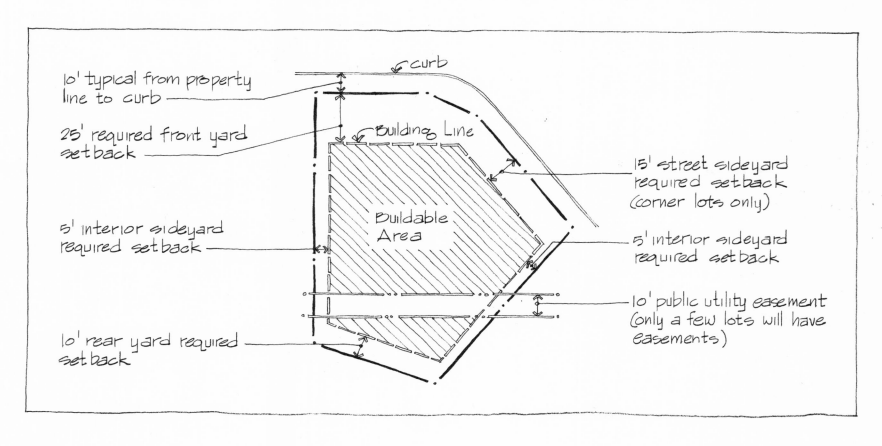

10' typical from property line to curb

25' required front yard setback

5' interior sideyard required setback

10' rear yard required setback

curb

Building Line

Buildable Area

15' street sideyard required setback (corner lots only)

5' interior sideyard required setback

10' public utility easement (only a few lots will have easements)

Site plot plans are usually drawn with an engineers scale and require an engineer's scale to de-code. Use one to scale off set-back requirements and easements on plot plan to determine the buildable area of the site.

Measure the buildable area and re-draw it at a larger architectural scale (1/8" or 1/4" scale) for planning your house. Also measure the trees on the site and any other important natural features and locate them on the site plan.

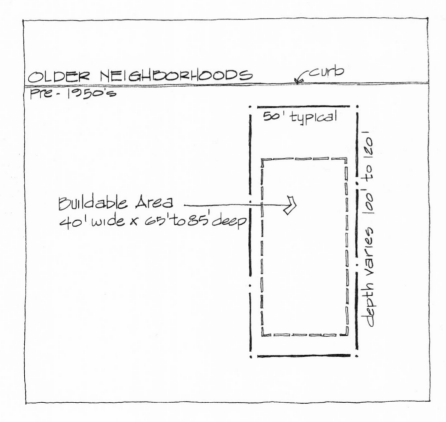

OLDER NEIGHBORHOODS

Pre-1950's

curb

50' typical

depth varies 100' to 120'

Buildable Area
40' wide x 65' to 85' deep

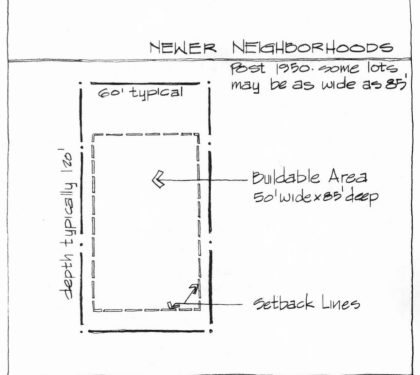

NEWER NEIGHBORHOODS

Post 1950. some lots may be as wide as 85'

60' typical

depth typically 120'

Buildable Area
50' wide x 85' deep

Setback Lines

SITE

SITE ANALYSIS NOTES

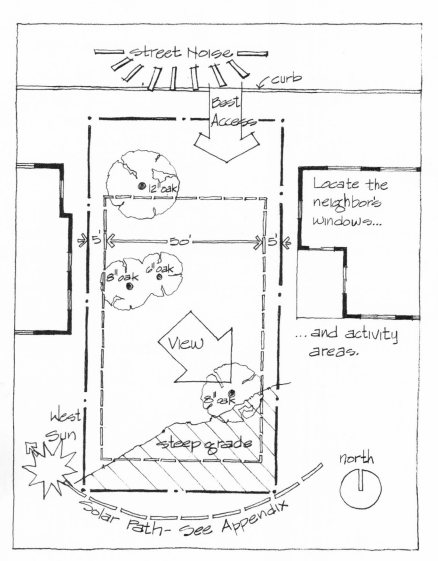

At this point, we should be able to draw a site plan and locate all the important factors pertinent to our design.

Physical factors include trees, neighboring structures, steep grades, solar orientation, wind directions, etc.

We should also note important psychological factors such as views, potential noise sources, neighbor's windows, etc.

Image labels: street Noise, curb, Best Access, 12"oak, Locate the neighbor's windows..., 5', 50', 5', 8"oak, 6"oak, View, ...and activity areas, West Sun, steep grade, 8"oak, Solar Path - See Appendix, north

PROGRAM

Designing the whole house at once may seem an awesome task given all the variables that must be considered and the inter-relationships arising between them in the design process. This procedure can be greatly simplified by first breaking the whole down into its parts and assigning a hierarchy or priority to some elements. This is what we do when we "program" a building. It is simply a list or menu of individual parts which will be included in the whole. In the design of a house, we can take each room and list the important features we desire of that space in our plan. This would include minimum dimensions and may include qualities such as orientation and proportions, as well as openings, furniture arrangements, shelves, and electrical outlets.

It will be advantageous to maintain some flexibility for the latter stages of planning, but this is our first step. Once we have a better knowledge of individual pieces, it will be much easier to put them all together in a meaningful way.

PROGRAM

A list or schedule like this one can help a designer think about each space in detail and write a better program.

space	user	use	adjacency	min. size	area	mood	light	walls	ceiling	floor	special consideration
foyer	public	reception	living & closet	5'x5'	25 sf	--	-	paint	paint	tile?	limited views into house
living	family	entertain	entry, bath dining	12'x14'	168 sf	informal	natural & indirect	paint	high & paint	area rugs on wood	view/fireplace/sunset
dining	family	eat	kitchen	10'x12'	120 sf	informal	natural	paint	paint	wood	view/fireplace
kitchen	family	cook	garage dining	8'x12'	96 sf	open	natural & fluorescent	paint	paint	tile	pantry serving/bkfst bar
mbr	mom & dad	relax, sleep read, tv	mbath	12'x12'	144 sf	cheerful	natural/ east sun	paint	paint	area rug on wood	morning sun, view privacy, quiet
br2	girl	study sleep	bath 2	10'x12'	120 sf	private	natural/ east sun	paint	paint	wood	morning sun
br3	boy	play sleep	bath 2	10'x12'	120 sf	fun	natural/ east sun	paint	paint	wood	morning sun
mbath	mom & dad	bath relax	mbedroom	6'x12'	72 sf	cheerful	natural	ceramic tile	paint	ceramic tile	window at whirlpool bath – walk-in-closet
bath 2	boy & girl	bath	br 2 & 3, living area	5'x8'	40 sf	clean	incand.	ceramic tile	paint	ceramic tile	functional
garage	autos	storage	kitchen	20'x20'	400 sf	functional	incand.	paint	exposed struct.	conc.	future workbench ping-pong table

Cars come in almost any size these days but for best resale value a garage should be at least 10' by 20' per car and wider if possible. Smaller garage doors are easier to handle and have a better architectural scale.

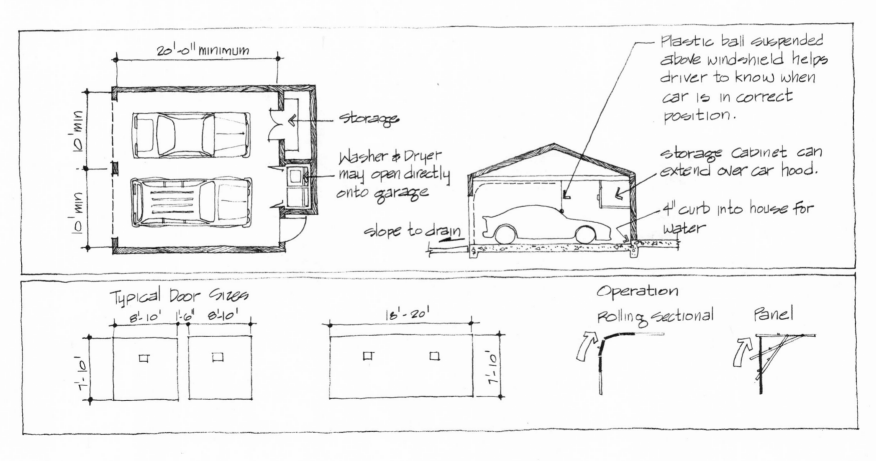

20'-0" minimum

10' min - 10' min

10' min

storage

Washer & Dryer may open directly onto garage

slope to drain

Plastic ball suspended above windshield helps driver to know when car is in correct position.

storage cabinet can extend over car hood.

4" curb into house for water

Typical Door Sizes

8'-10' 1'-6" 8'-10'

7'-10'

18'-20'

7'-10'

Operation

Rolling sectional   Panel

PROGRAM

BEDROOM

Minimum bedroom dimension should not be less than 10 feet, and each bedroom must have visual as well as acoustical privacy from the more active areas of the house. We can lay out the proper bed and night stand sizes to determine width. Length will depend on circulation, type and locations of closets, seating areas, etc.

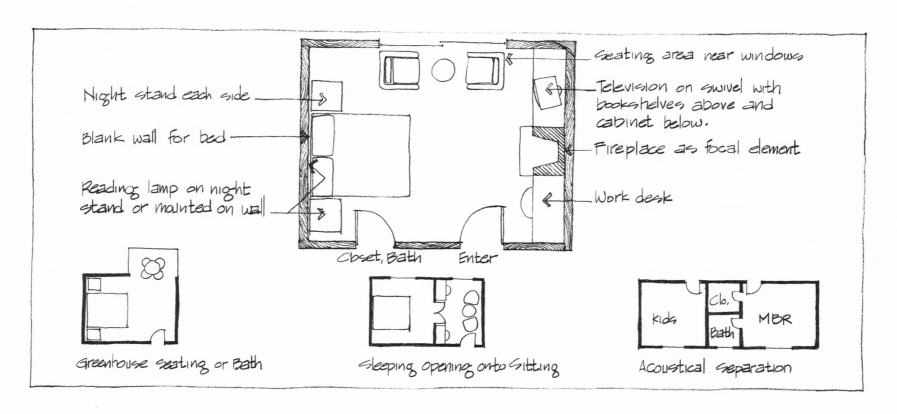

Night stand each side

Blank wall for bed

Reading lamp on night stand or mounted on wall

Seating area near windows

Television on swivel with bookshelves above and cabinet below.

Fireplace as focal element

Work desk

Closet, Bath   Enter

Greenhouse Seating or Bath

Sleeping opening onto Sitting

Acoustical Separation

Kids   Clo.   Bath   MBR

9'-0" can be considered a minimum width for a dining room allowing for a table width of 33" to 36" and a minimum of 3'-0" each side for seating and circulation. Minimum room length can be found by taking the table length and adding 3' to each end.

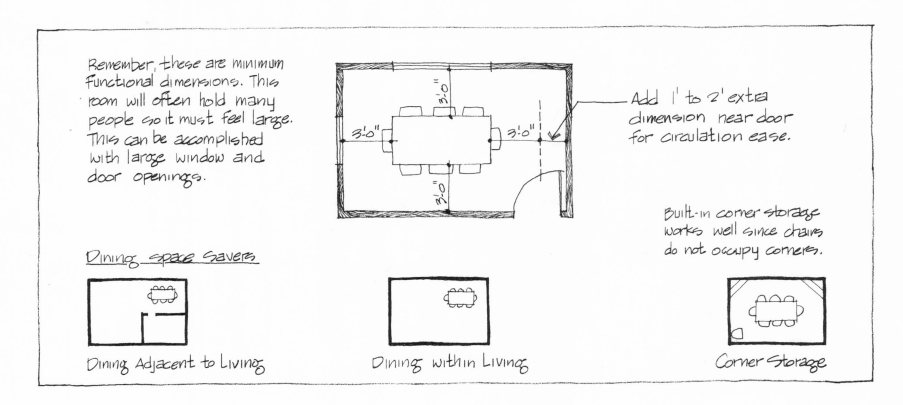

Remember, these are minimum functional dimensions. This room will often hold many people so it must feel large. This can be accomplished with large window and door openings.

Add 1' to 2' extra dimension near door for circulation ease.

Built-in corner storage works well since chairs do not occupy corners.

Dining Space Savers

Dining Adjacent to Living

Dining within Living

Corner Storage

25

PROGRAM

KITCHEN

8'-0" is a minimum dimension for a 'pullman' type kitchen. All appliances will fit into a 2'-0" deep counter space and individual widths are as noted on plan below.

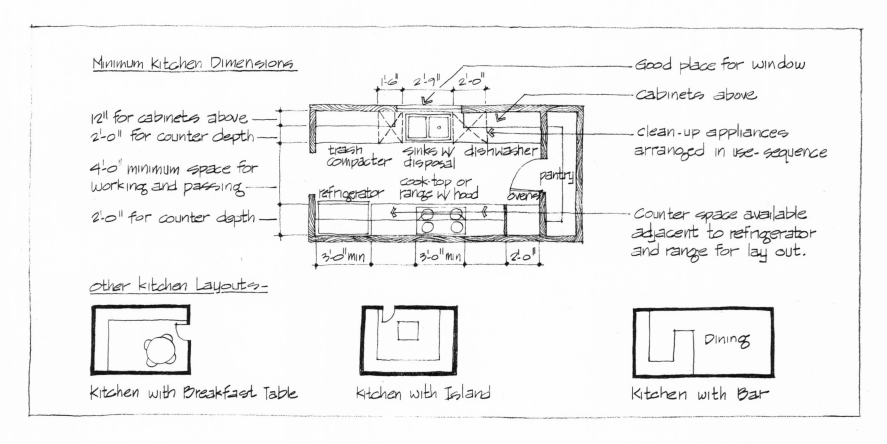

Minimum Kitchen Dimensions

12" for cabinets above
2'-0" for counter depth

4'-0" minimum space for working and passing

2'-0" for counter depth

1'-6" 2'-9" 2'-0"

trash compacter   sinks w/ disposal   dishwasher

refrigerator   cook-top or range w/ hood   oven   pantry

3'-0" min   3'-0" min   2'-0"

Good place for window

cabinets above

clean-up appliances arranged in use-sequence

Counter space available adjacent to refrigerator and range for lay out.

Other Kitchen Layouts—

Kitchen with Breakfast Table

Kitchen with Island

Dining

Kitchen with Bar

The best way to size a living area is to first determine its uses. We can start with a minimum size of 12 feet by 14 feet and lay out furniture to comply with our uses. Special consideration must be given to focal elements such as television or fireplace and maintaining intimacy of conversation groupings.

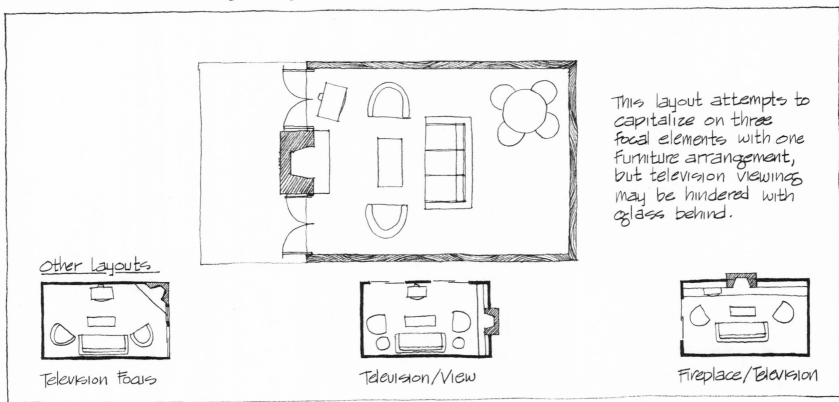

This layout attempts to capitalize on three focal elements with one furniture arrangement, but television viewing may be hindered with glass behind.

Other Layouts

Television Focus

Television/View

Fireplace/Television

27

PROGRAM

BATHROOM

In general, each toilet fixture requires 2'-6" minimum width and 5'-0" clear, front wall to rear wall. This gives a minimum size for a full bath as 7'-6" by 5'-0" inside dimensions. Money can be saved by keeping all the plumbing in one wall. Having established the minimum standards, we should note that a large bathroom can be a true pleasure.

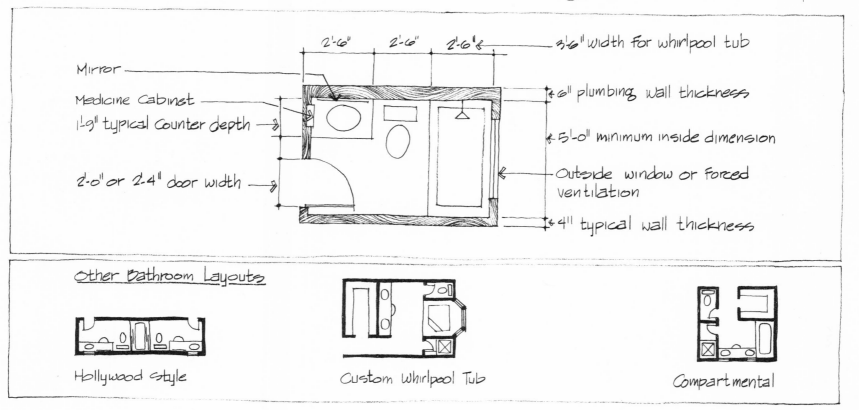

2'-6"   2'-6"   2'-6"   3'-6" width for whirlpool tub

Mirror

Medicine Cabinet   6" plumbing wall thickness

1'-9" typical Counter depth   5'-0" minimum inside dimension

2'-0" or 2-4" door width   Outside window or forced ventilation

                                        4" typical wall thickness

Other Bathroom Layouts

Hollywood Style   Custom Whirlpool Tub   Compartmental

Residential washer and dryers are available in the standard types and sizes plus many new compact space saver sizes and concepts.

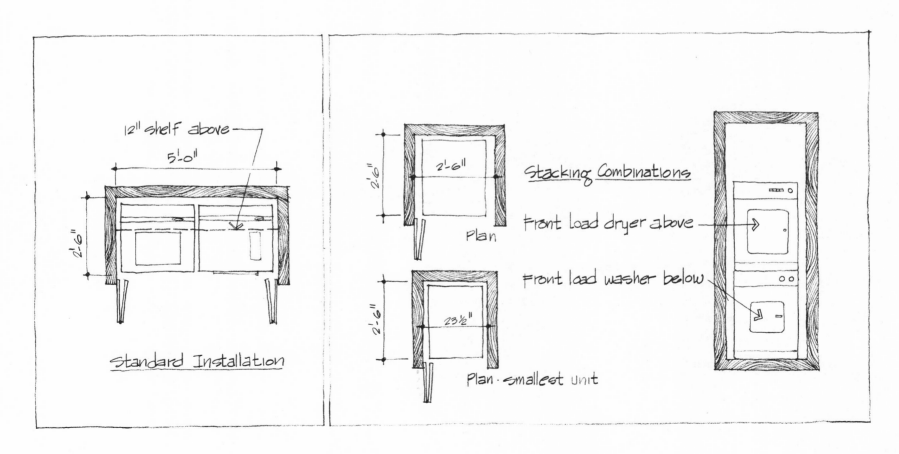

12" shelf above

5'-0"

2'-6"

Standard Installation

Stacking Combinations

2'-6"

2'-6"

Plan

2'-6"

23½"

Plan · smallest unit

Front load dryer above

Front load washer below

PROGRAM

MECHANICAL

Central heat and/or air conditioning requires a small compartment within the house for the fan mechanism called the air handler. This should be in a central location for proper air return and supply. It can be in a closet for a vertical air handler or in an attic space for a horizontal unit.

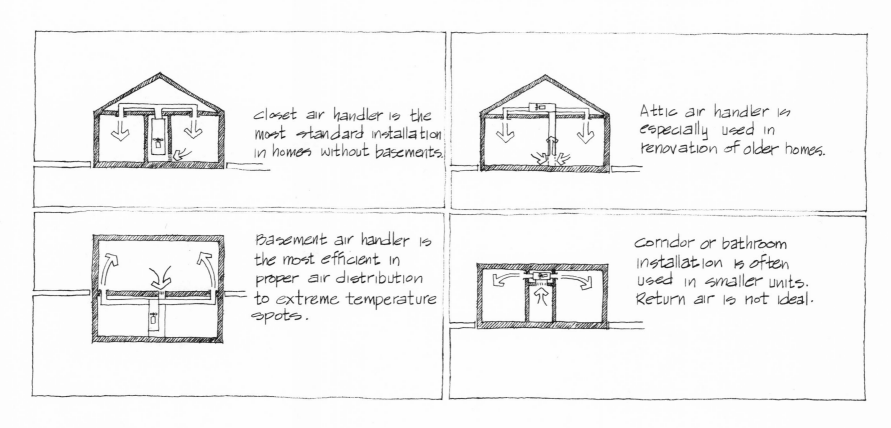

closet air handler is the most standard installation in homes without basements.

Attic air handler is especially used in renovation of older homes.

Basement air handler is the most efficient in proper air distribution to extreme temperature spots.

Corridor or bathroom installation is often used in smaller units. Return air is not ideal.

Three rules to remember when designing locations
for fan unit and air grilles:

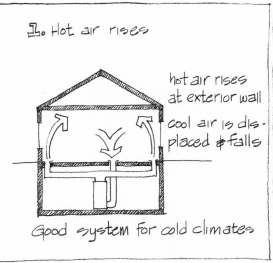

1. Hot air rises

hot air rises
at exterior wall

Cool air is dis-
placed & falls

Good system for cold climates

2. Cold air falls and settles

Coolest air falls at exterior
walls. Cool air at floor
is recirculated.
Good system for hot climates

3. Air ducts are best located
where they are most needed.

Glass is a poor
insulator....

outside
temperature
extreme

The area just inside an
opening will be an un-
comfortable interior
zone. Good design
practice is to handle
temperature spots in
the most direct manner.

Zoning - Houses may be zoned with dampers for energy
conservation in little used areas during temperature
extremes. Larger houses may have two separate
air handlers for complete zoning.

PROGRAM

MECHANICAL

The hot water heater generally requires a closet (ventilated. if gas-fired) best located near a plumbing wall for cost efficiency. The closer to the outlet, the sooner it arrives. Air handlers (heating unit/a.c.fan) should be placed in a central location to reduce length of duct runs.

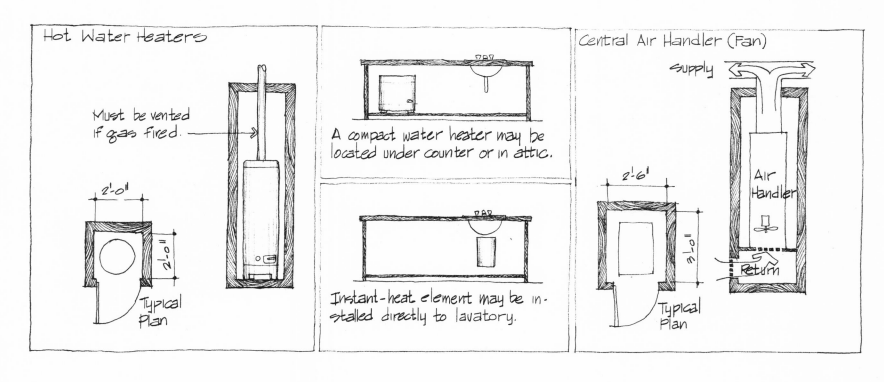

Hot Water Heaters

Must be vented if gas fired.

2'-0"

2'-0"

Typical Plan

A compact water heater may be located under counter or in attic.

Instant-heat element may be installed directly to lavatory.

Central Air Handler (Fan)

Supply

Air Handler

2'-6"

3'-0"

Return

Typical Plan

Closet sizes depend upon what is being stored.
Clothes require a minimum of 2'-0" depth.

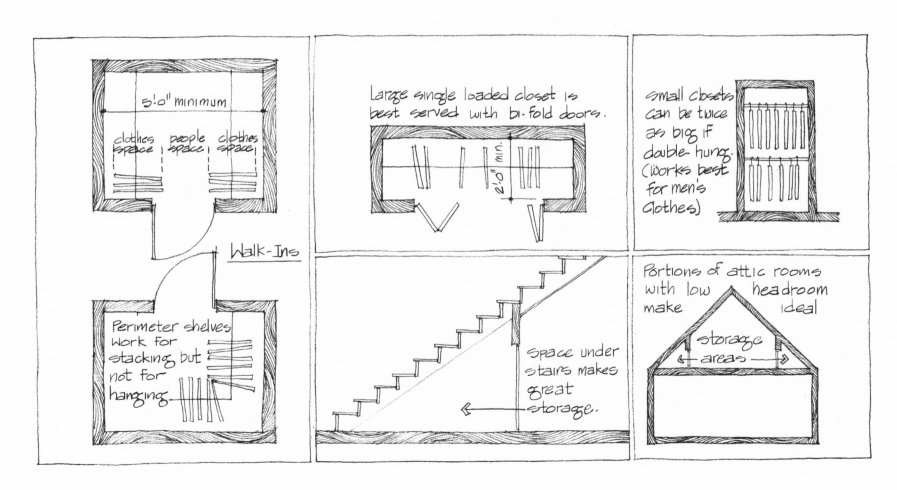

5'-0" minimum

clothes space | people space | clothes space

Walk-Ins

Perimeter shelves work for stacking but not for hanging.

Large single loaded closet is best served with bi-fold doors.

2'-0" min.

Small closets can be twice as big if double-hung. (works best for men's clothes)

Space under stairs makes great storage.

Portions of attic rooms with low headroom make ideal storage areas

PROGRAM

STAIRS

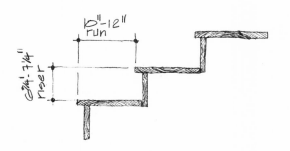

Minimum residential stair width should be 3'-0" for two way circulation. Handrail must be 33" above stair nosing. Riser height should be between 6¾" and 7¼" and run between 10" and 12". A spiral stair cannot be counted as an 'exit' by code, therefore should not serve sleeping areas.

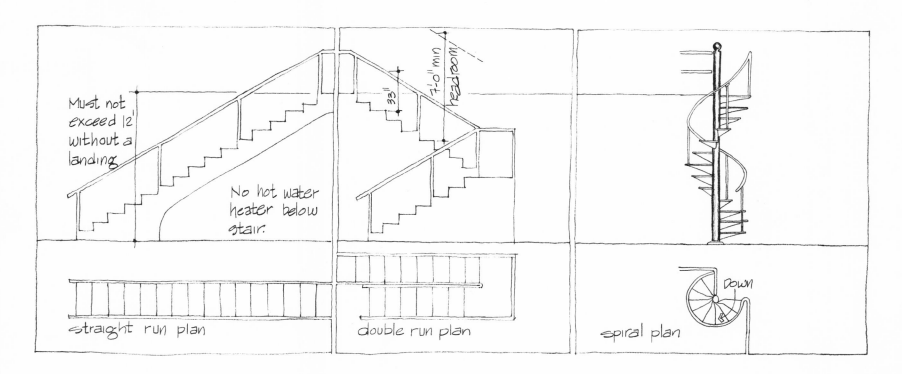

Must not exceed 12' without a landing

No hot water heater below stair.

33"

7'-0" min. headroom

straight run plan

double run plan

spiral plan

Down

PLAN

Now that we have studied the individual parts, it is time to put them together. This chapter shows two basic methods to accomplish this feat. The preferred method is explained in a step-by-step analysis using the site and program from the previous chapters. It is literally as easy to follow as cutting out paper dolls. Of course we must give some thought to over-all area (which is money), zoning (which can mean a peaceful nights sleep, and size (which is also money), or apparent size (which is not money). This process is then subjected to some amount of pushing and pulling to mesh the parts The end result will be a plan that works well with your site and your program. Then more pushing and pulling as we test it for elevation compatibility.

PLAN

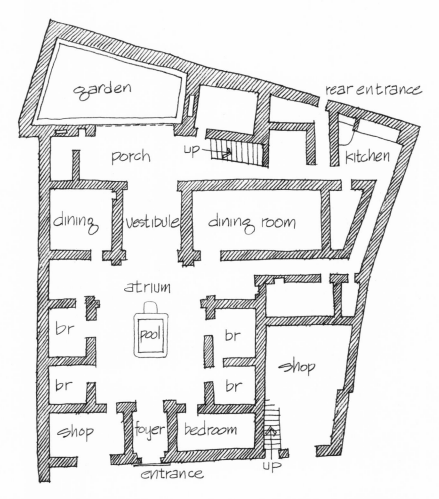

garden

rear entrance

porch

up

kitchen

dining | vestibule | dining room

atrium

pool

br | br | shop

br | br

shop | foyer | bedroom | up

entrance

PLAN OF THE HOUSE OF THE SURGEON, POMPEII
from Vitruvius

A building plan is the view one would have of a building if one were able to make a horizontal cut across the whole structure about 4 feet above the floor, lift off the top and peer down into the bottom.

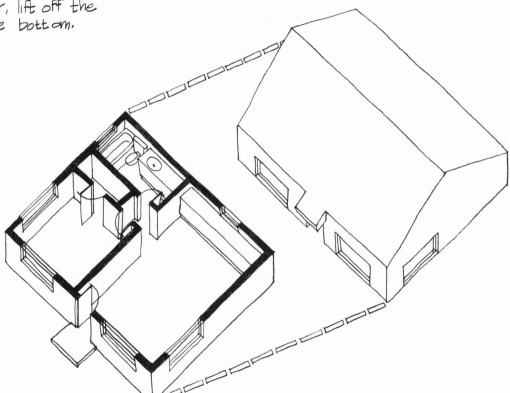

Walls are usually denoted with thick dark lines. Windows are usually three parallel lines and doors are shown open with an arc to denote the swing.

PLAN

COST vs. AREA

Complex Plan, Expensive Materials
$75⁰⁰ per square foot

Simple Plan, Inexpensive Materials
$25⁰⁰ per square foot

Before we begin the actual design, it would be helpful to set some area guidelines and determine how much house we can afford to build. A quick reference to the chapter on FINANCE (pp. 123) will give us an idea of what amount we can borrow for construction.

Let's say our local Savings and Loan will loan us $145,000 based on our income and long-term debts. Our 10% down payment of $15,000 gives us a total of $160,000 for land and construction. Assuming $70,000 for the cost of the lot, we are left with $90,000 for construction.

Carports and other semi-finished areas can be counted at one-half value. Let's assume that $45.00 per square foot of finished house is a good median price range for our purpose.

Total Money Available	$90,000.⁰⁰
2 car garage (20'x20' x $22.50/sf)	-9,000.⁰⁰
Amount left for house	$81,000.⁰⁰

$81,000. ÷ $45.⁰⁰/sf = 1800 square feet finished area

1800 sf x 75% = 1350 square feet programed area.

A zoning plan establishes the basic layout by defining the major spaces and their preferred adjacent spaces.

A house has public and private areas and these are usually separated acoustically and physically for more comfortable living.

Of course the exterior wall area is a major contributor to the overall cost, so we must make the plan more compact once we have determined our zoning priorities.

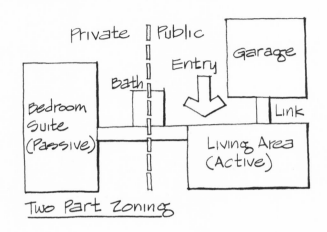

Two Part Zoning

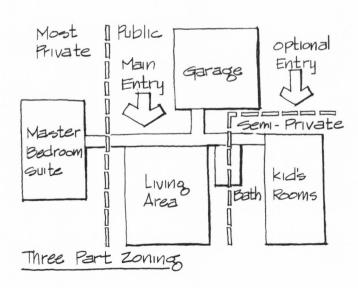

Three Part Zoning

PLAN

OPEN PLAN VS. CLOSED PLAN

Many people prefer separate living functions to be contained within distinctly separate spaces. This closed plan concept has a great deal of merit; however it generally describes a larger and therefore more expensive house. The 'open plan concept' for the more active functions, means separate functional areas can share a large space. This allows a feeling of expanse within the framework of a smaller house.

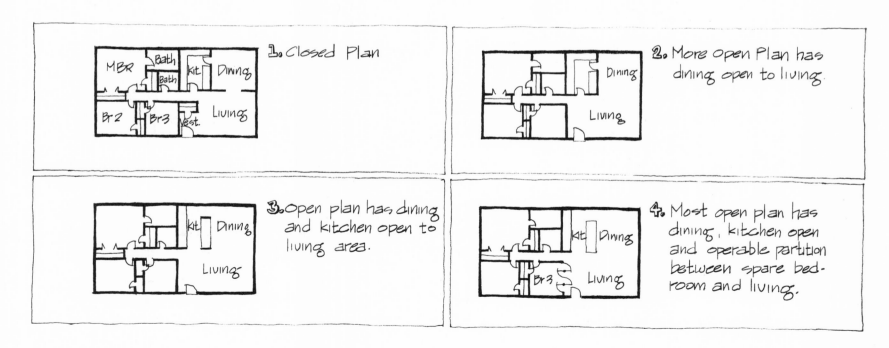

1. Closed Plan

2. More open plan has dining open to living.

3. Open plan has dining and kitchen open to living area.

4. Most open plan has dining, kitchen open and operable partition between spare bedroom and living.

SUBTRACTIVE PLAN

There are two methods of attack to the plan. The first can be called the subtractive process. It is similar to the way we arrived at the 'buildable area' on our site plan. We start with a preconceived exterior shape (which fits into our site plan) and sub-divide it into the individual rooms. Gridded paper to scale, such as 1/8" graph paper, is a good background for this method.

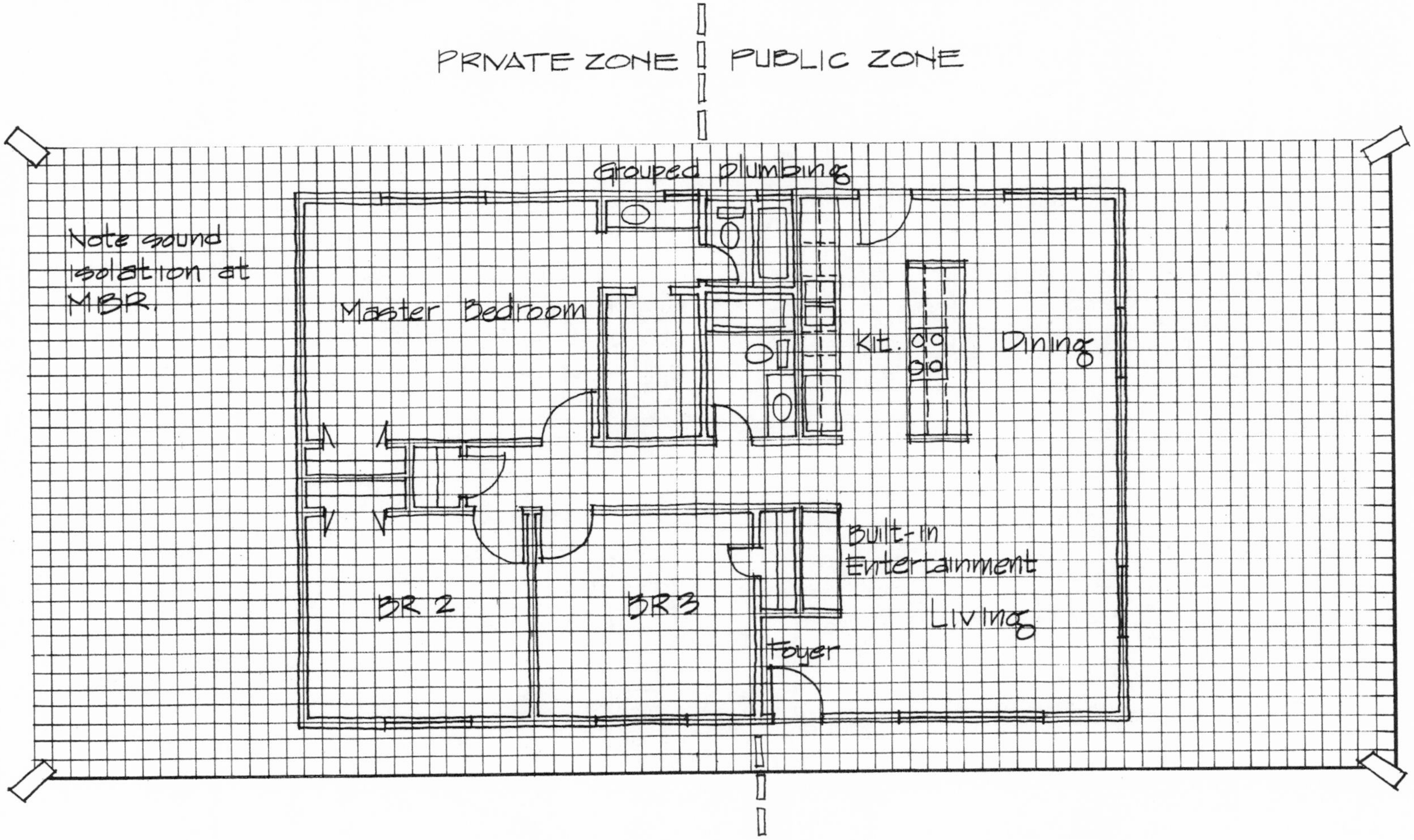

PRIVATE ZONE | PUBLIC ZONE

Grouped plumbing

Note sound isolation at MBR.

Master Bedroom

Kit.   Dining

Built-in Entertainment

BR 2   BR 3   Living

Foyer

41

PLAN

PROGRAM PARTS

Garage
20' x 20'
400 SF

Living
14' x 20'
280 SF

The other method commonly used by architects is the additive method. In this method we first roughly design the smaller elements, draw them to the same scale as our site plan (¼" or ⅛"), and cut them out.

Dining
10' x 12'
120 SF

Kitchen
8' x 12'
96 SF

Consult the section on individual rooms for minimum dimensions, clearances, etc. for each room. Also make sure the total area of the rooms is about 75% of our total area budget, because we still must add in storage and circulation space.

Master Bedroom
12' x 16'
192 SF

BR 2
11' x 12'
132 SF

BR 3
10' x 12'
120 SF

Master Bath
10' x 6'

Bath 2
8' x 6'

The next step is to move the cut-outs around on the site plan until they seem to be in the right place with respect to the other rooms and the site itself. We only concern ourselves with the major spaces at this point. The appurtenant spaces such as corridors and closets will be worked into the in-between spaces later. Make sure that all rooms needing outside windows have an exterior wall.

If we are designing a multi-story house, it is important that stairs, fireplace chimneys, etc. line up for vertical connection, and that some walls line up for structural support to the roof. See TRANSFORMER chapter, p.p. 91, for an example.

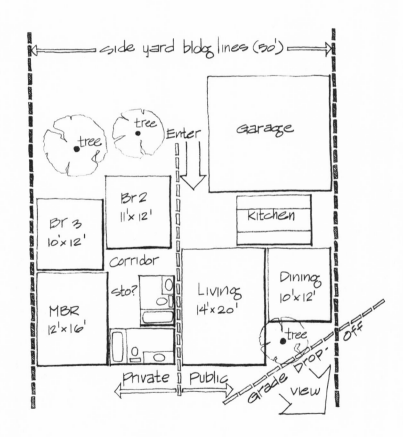

PLAN

When we are satisfied that we have the rooms in good order, it may be necessary to shift or reshape them slightly to form a more cohesive plan. We can lay a piece of tracing paper over our cut-outs and sketch the changes, stretching here, compacting there, adding corridors and storage space as we search for order.

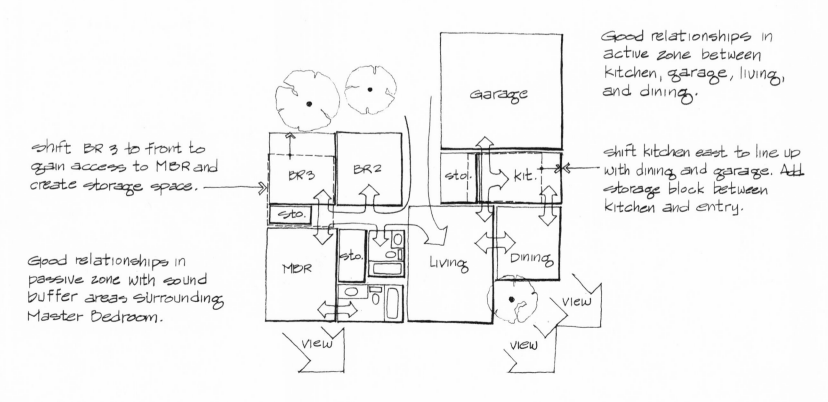

Good relationships in active zone between kitchen, garage, living, and dining.

shift kitchen east to line up with dining and garage. Add storage block between kitchen and entry.

shift BR 3 to front to gain access to MBR and create storage space.

Good relationships in passive zone with sound buffer areas surrounding Master Bedroom.

44

The next overlay will be further refinements and adjustments for access, storage, and order. This means lining up walls that are close, sub-dividing storage areas, and checking access at secondary spaces.

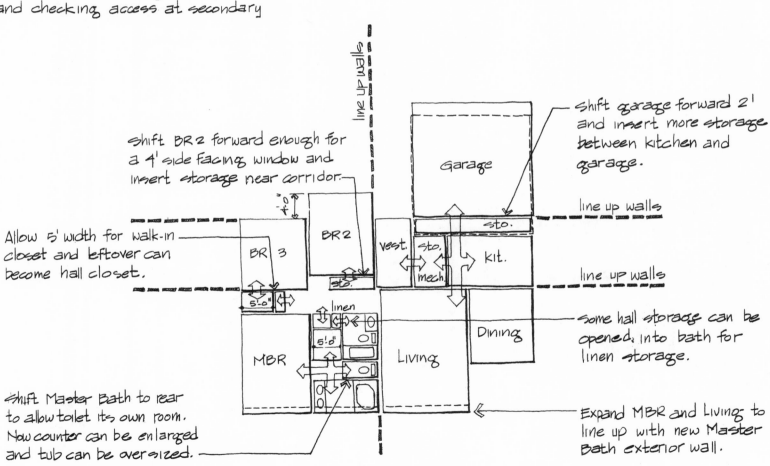

line up walls

Shift garage forward 2' and insert more storage between kitchen and garage.

Garage

Shift BR2 forward enough for a 4' side facing window and insert storage near corridor.

line up walls

BR 2

Allow 5' width for walk-in closet and leftover can become hall closet.

BR 3

vest.   sto.

kit.

sto.

mech.

line up walls

sto.

5'-0"

linen

Some hall storage can be opened into bath for linen storage.

5'-0"

MBR

Living

Dining

Shift Master Bath to rear to allow toilet its own room. Now counter can be enlarged and tub can be oversized.

Expand MBR and Living to line up with new Master Bath exterior wall.

PLAN

REFINING

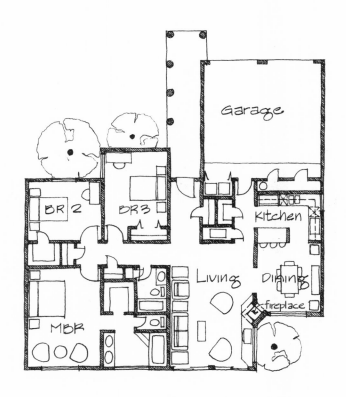

After a series of overlay refinements we will arrive at a plan that seems to satisfy our basic requirements in terms of room sizes, storage areas, zoning, and efficiency. Now we must test it for our particular lifestyle by laying out the openings, furniture, and appliances in each room. This becomes very important in the case of focal elements such as fire-places, televisions, or major art pieces.

If the furniture layout works, we can add details such as electrical out-lets, switches, telephone jacks, cable TV jacks, stereo speaker jacks, etc. See the section on individual rooms for help.

Before we can congratulate ourselves on designing the perfect plan, we must test it with elevation studies.

ELEVATIONS

If our plan is perfect it should draw its own elevation, or at least suggest it. This chapter takes us step-by-step through the sometimes arduous task of elevation studies. Like the plan, the elevation requires juggling several variables until some recede, allowing others to receive more concentrated attention. More than any other problem in the design process, the elevations are done on a trial and error basis. Blocking out the first elevations from the plan initiates a back and forth exchange between plan and elevation, pushing a wall in here or pulling one out over there in order to arrive at the desired massing.

This chapter is presented here for continuity. However, it will be better understood after reading the chapters on AESTHETIC DESIGN (massing and composition) and STYLE.

Refer to these chapters before you draw.

ELEVATIONS

A building elevation is the view one would have if one were able to look at the facade of a structure straight-on, perpendicular, without any distortion of the perspective view.

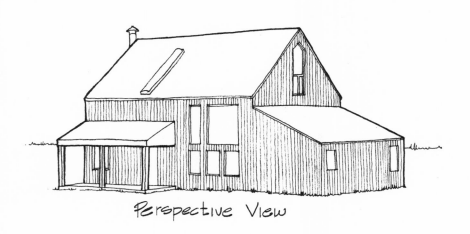

Perspective View

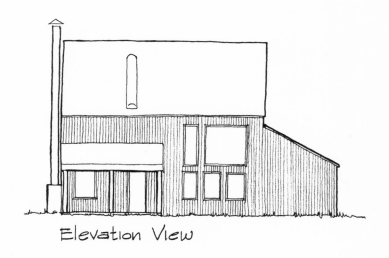

Elevation View

After a house at Sea Ranch by MLT/Moore & Turnbull

This technical view allows the designer to scale, compose, and describe more exactly what is happening on each face of the building.

The elevations will be easier to understand and to draw if we first study the building section. This is the view one would have if one were able to make a vertical cut through the structure and look inside.

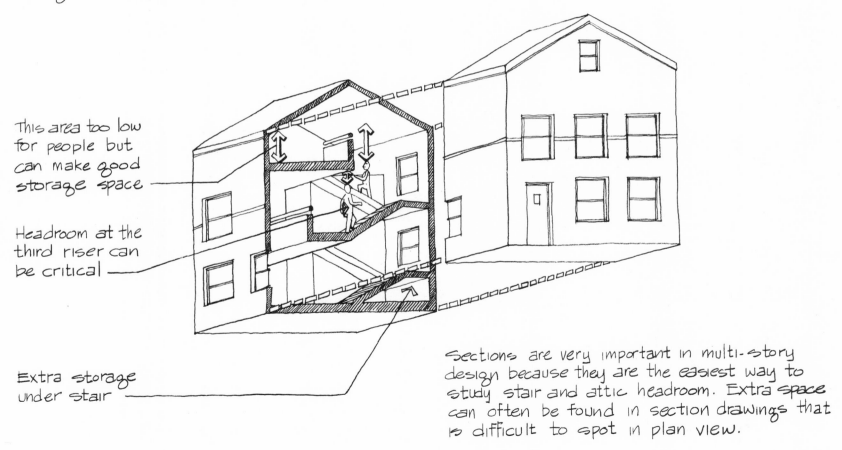

This area too low for people but can make good storage space

Headroom at the third riser can be critical

Extra storage under stair

Sections are very important in multi-story design because they are the easiest way to study stair and attic headroom. Extra space can often be found in section drawings that is difficult to spot in plan view.

49

ELEVATIONS

SECTIONS

Sections are the best drawings to describe construction methods and materials, especially those things hidden by wall or ceiling sheathing.

A section drawing is often the easiest way to describe a complex detail to a contractor or carpenter.

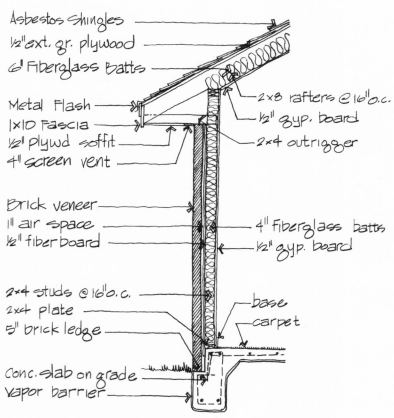

Asbestos Shingles
½" ext. gr. plywood
6' Fiberglass batts

Metal Flash
1x10 Fascia
½" plywd soffit
4" screen vent

2x8 rafters @ 16" o.c.
½" gyp. board
2x4 outrigger

Brick veneer
1" air space
½" fiberboard

4" Fiberglass batts
½" gyp. board

2x4 studs @ 16" o.c.
2x4 plate
5" brick ledge

base
carpet

Conc. slab on grade
vapor barrier

TYPICAL WALL SECTION

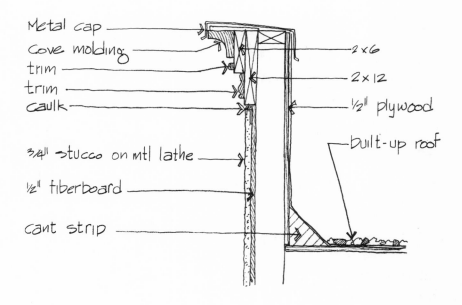

Metal cap
Cove molding
trim
trim
caulk

2x6
2x12
½" plywood
built-up roof

¾" stucco on mtl lathe

½" fiberboard

cant strip

DETAIL SECTION

Setting the necessary height parameters to begin elevation drawings will only require a simple sketch section. The most important of these is the plate height of the wall, which is the vertical measure from the floor to the top of the "plate," that portion of the wall the roof or floor frame rests upon.

When we draw the elevation we must compensate for the slope of over-hangs in the drawing.

plate

8'-1"

Finish floor
plate

8'-1"

Finish floor

STRUCTURAL SECTION

The plate height is usually 8'-1" in most residential construction since gypsum board and plywood come in 8'-0" lengths. It can be any height we desire, however, with some loss in economy.

51

ELEVATIONS

The tops of windows and doors, called the "head height," must also be established. The standard height for residential doors is 6'-8". In general, the tops of windows are made even with the doors. Taller doors and windows can easily be had at some slight increase in cost.

sill height

2'-6" to 3'-0"

plate height

head height

8'-1"

6'-8"

Finish floor level

sill heights above 3'-0" will be uncomfortably high when seated inside and looking out.

The basic method for constructing an elevation is to lay a piece of tracing paper over the floor plan, establish finish floor lines, plate heights and head heights, and begin projecting wall, window, door, and roof elements onto the blocked-out elevation.

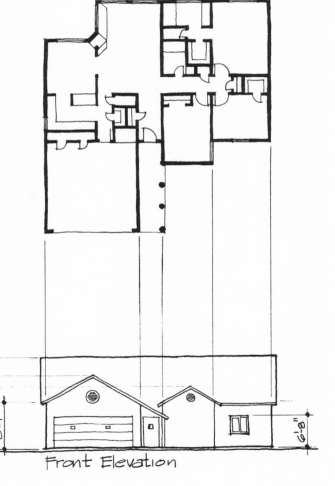

A rough side elevation sketch alongside the front elevation helps project proper roof and overhang heights.

plate line

finish floor line

Side Elevation

Front Elevation

8'-0"

6'-8"

ELEVATIONS

ROOF TYPES...

Before we make the first pass at an elevation, it would be helpful to make a roof plan as a direction for the elevation study. We have a choice of a flat roof (with or without parapet), a sloped roof, or any combination. In general, the less complex the roof design, the less likely it is to leak.

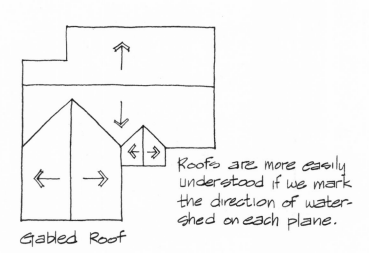

Roofs are more easily understood if we mark the direction of water-shed on each plane.

Gabled Roof

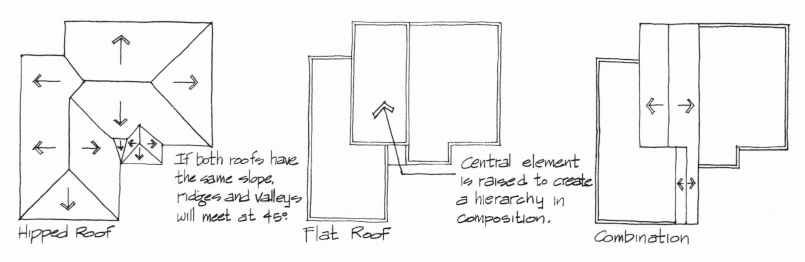

If both roofs have the same slope, ridges and valleys will meet at 45°.

Hipped Roof

Central element is raised to create a hierarchy in composition.

Flat Roof

Combination

We should sketch out two or three roof plans and block out the main elevations of each to find a primary direction. We can also play with changing roof slopes and plate heights as variations on each scheme. Refer to the section on architectural style for characteristic design elements representational of the particular periods.

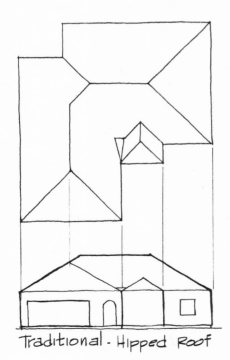

Traditional · Hipped Roof

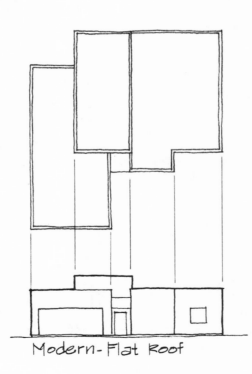

Modern · Flat Roof

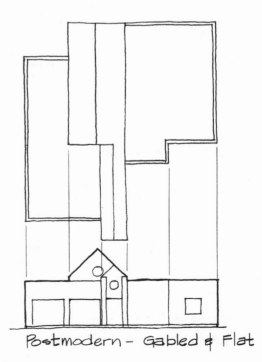

Postmodern · Gabled & Flat

ELEVATIONS

When we find an elevation direction we want to pursue, we must block out all the faces of the building in the same way, adding detail as we go.

At this point we can study minor plan modifications such as moving or adding windows, projecting some plan element out to better define the elevation, detaching the garage from the house, etc.

project porch

add windows

Front Elevation

Side Elevation

This series of elevations seem successful. The simple, uncomplex design has an inherent elegance that gives presence to this relatively small house. The windows have shifted and the repetition of square openings add cohesion to the whole.

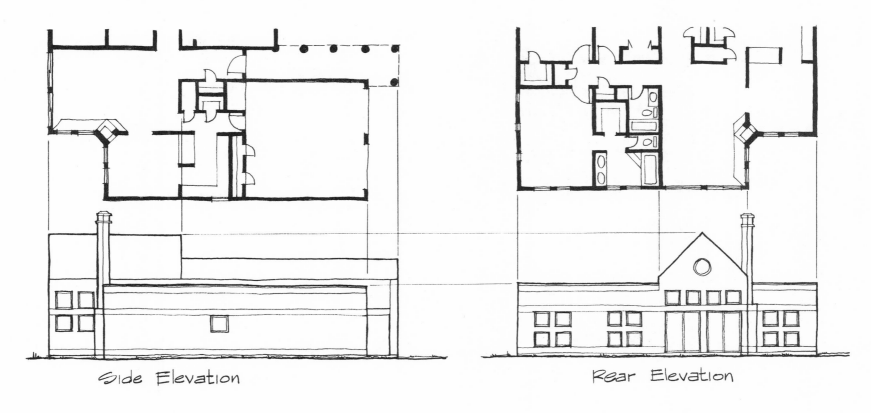

Side Elevation

Rear Elevation

ELEVATIONS

INTERIOR ELEVATIONS

Just as we must draw exterior elevations to show a contractor exactly what we want the house to look like on the outside, we must also draw elevations of those interior walls that are important to us. These would include kitchen cabinets, bathroom cabinets, any special shelves and/or cabinets, special moldings, openings, or paint schemes.

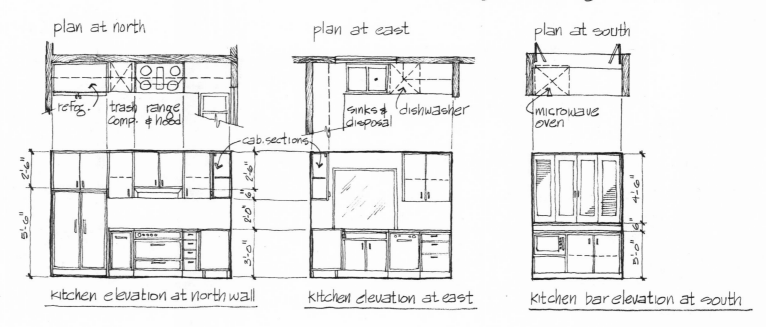

plan at north

plan at east

plan at south

refg.

trash range
comp. & hood

sinks & disposal

dishwasher

microwave oven

cab. sections

kitchen elevation at north wall

kitchen elevation at east

kitchen bar elevation at south

Be sure to show important dimensions and note any special materials, details, or equipment on these drawings.

MODEL

After the elevations are refined to a certain point we are ready to begin the model. This exercise is probably the most fun and revealing of all for the designer because it takes the building from two-dimensional drawings to a three-dimensional object.

Again, as in elevation studies, we should not concern ourselves with getting it perfect the first time. Design is a process of communication between the designer and the design with information constantly passing in both directions.

The techniques of model making may seem clumsy at first but they are quickly learned. with a little practice and the final model should be much more craftsmanlike than the first. The important thing in model building, like all design processes, is to begin with the first step and not be overwhelmed by the complexity of the total problem.

MODEL

Building a scale model of the house is by far the best way to visualize the total design in three dimensions. The process of building the model also helps us to think about our design within the construction sequence. We may also uncover hidden usable spaces which were difficult to visualize in two-dimensional drawings.

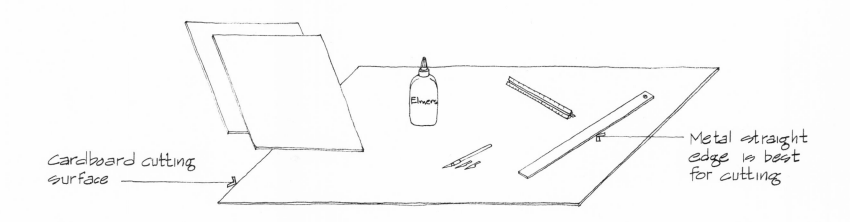

Cardboard cutting surface

Metal straight edge is best for cutting

There are many difficult types and scales of models to chose from, but for our purposes a fairly large scale interior and exterior model with a lift-off roof would best help us understand our design. We can build this type of model with cardboard, art board (or even stiff paper), an exacto knife, and Elmer's Glue.

For convenience, we decide to build the model at a scale of 1/4"=1'-0" since our drawings are already at this scale. Next, we select a board thick enough to be strong at this size but thin enough to be cut easily, such as bristol board. To begin, we can make a print or xerox of our floor plan to glue onto the board (or copy the plan directly onto the board).

Place straight edge on inside of plan to protect it and make several weak passes until knife is finally through the material.

Cut around the outside edges of the plan and we have the model floor plate.

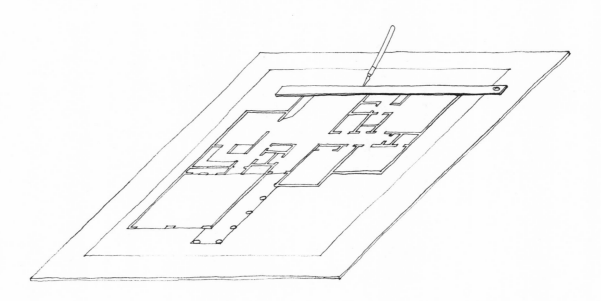

MODEL

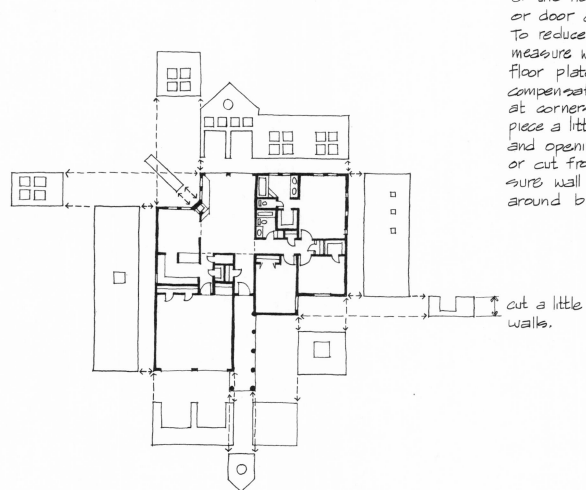

Next, cut out each exterior wall of the house and each window or door opening in that wall. To reduce the possibility of error, measure wall length directly from floor plate. Don't forget to compensate for board thickness at corners by cutting sandwiched piece a little short. Wall heights and openings can be measured or cut from elevations. Make sure wall heights are consistant around building.

cut a little short to fit between walls.

Test each wall for accurate length and height before applying glue. Errors tend to amplify themselves as you go, so it is very important to keep any errors within each individual wall.

Glue each wall into place with a minimum amount of glue. This can be best done by placing a small amount of glue on a piece of paper and using a small cardboard daub to apply it to the bottom and sides of each wall. This allows the glue to set fast and allows easy removal of walls later for changes or corrections.

If you want to remove a wall, make a light cut with the knife around the base of the wall and gently rock it back and forth until it breaks free.

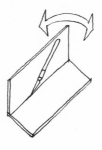

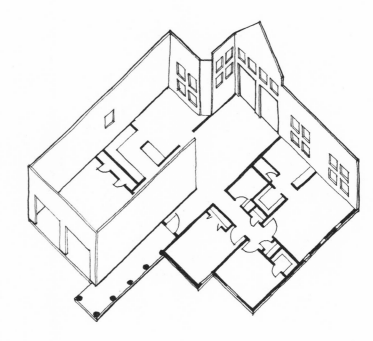

MODEL

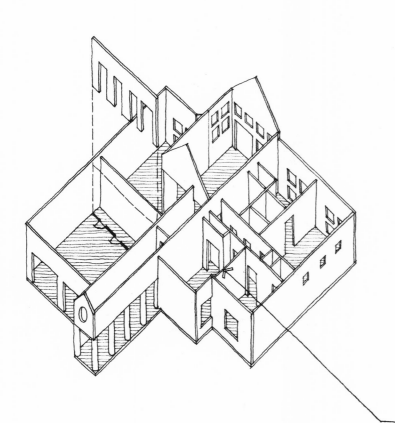

Once the exterior walls are in place we can begin on the interior partitions. Measure each length on the actual model to control the degree of error due to cardboard thickness, etc. Each wall should be glued in place before cutting the next one to insure proper fit.

Now we have a fairly accurate representation of the volume and proportion of each space. Placing the model at the corresponding solar to an ordinary light source will give a good indication of the amount and quality of the natural light in the various rooms. It will also allow accurate design of any shading devices or overhangs.

Interior walls are cut shorter than exterior walls to allow for parapet when roof is attached.

Once we have the model complete, we can use the walls for templates to cut colored Pantone Paper, and apply the colored paper to each wall. This helps us to accurately study color schemes and light in each space and on the exterior.

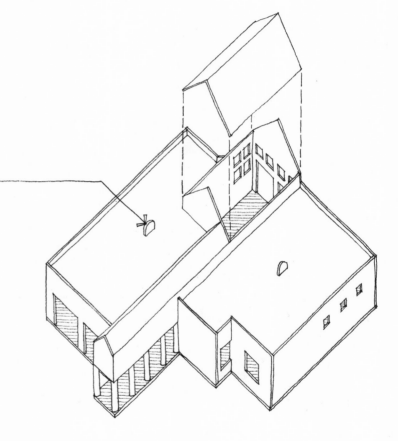

Axonometric View

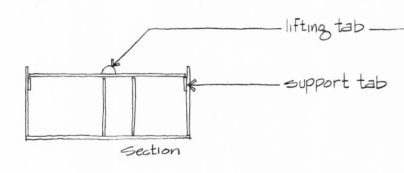

lifting tab

support tab

Section

Flat roofs can be cut exactly like the floor plate, except slightly smaller to allow for wall thickness if there is a parapet. Glue tabs onto the walls for support and one on the roof for lifting-off.

MODEL

SLOPED ROOFS

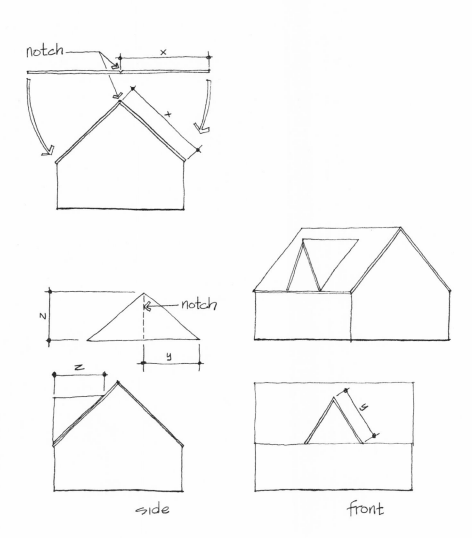

notch

x

+

notch

z

y

z

s

side

front

A sloped roof is slightly difficult since it fits on the model at an angle. We can measure the length of the gable to determine how wide to cut the board. If we cut both sides of the gable on one piece and then lightly notch the ridge, the roof will fold nicely along the notch and be easier to handle.

Intersections between two sloping roofs can be more difficult. Length 'y' can be taken from the front elevation and length 'z' taken from the side elevation to construct the proper cut as shown. More difficult pieces can be formed by trial and error, using paper patterns until the fit is correct and then transferred to cardboard.

PERSPECTIVE

There are as many difficult methods to perspective drawing as there drawing instructors. This chapter represents a distillation of several methods into a step-by-step process for simple massing. In general, perspective drawing is not as good a tool for design studies as a model because it is time consuming, is limited to a view from one point in space, and can be easily distorted. It is usually used as a promotional tool for a finished design and can make the building appear more real than a simple model.
It is included here because the drawing construction can be fun and the process helps explain some spatial concepts to the designer.

PERSPECTIVE

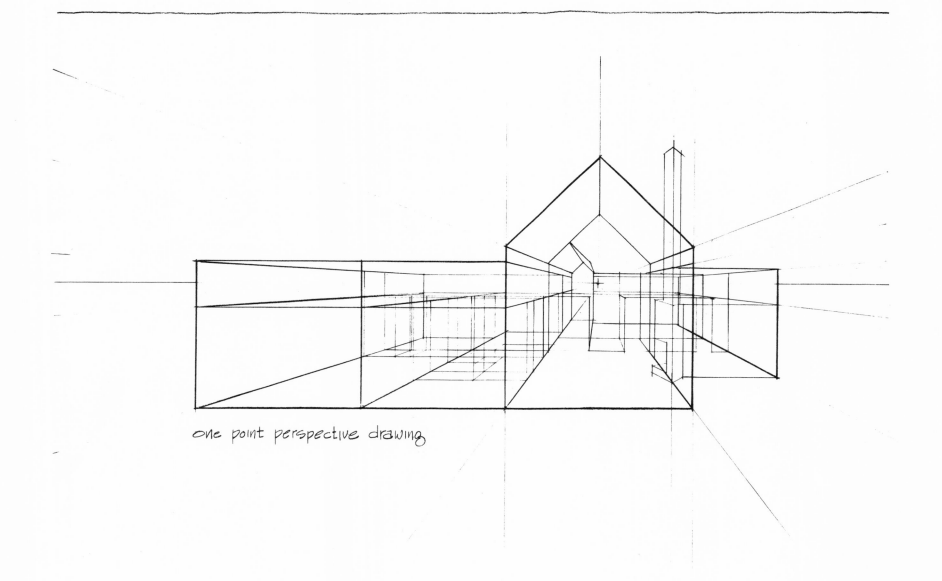

one point perspective drawing

Although good perspective drawing requires
practice, the rules are simple and can be
applied by anyone with a little patience.
The following is a step-by-step construction
of an accurately scaled two-point perspective
drawing from a plan.

1. Place plan on table at
correct angle of view.

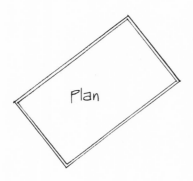

Plan

View Desired

2. Draw the 'picture plane' line through the
foremost corner of the plan.

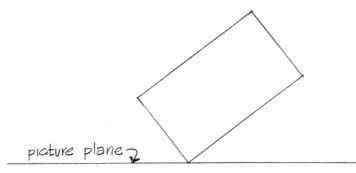

picture plane

PERSPECTIVE

3. Draw the 'vertical measure' line through the foremost corner of the plan.

4. The 'station point' is that point at which the viewer stands to look at the plan. Pick the station point so that a 60° angle from that point will encompass the whole plan.

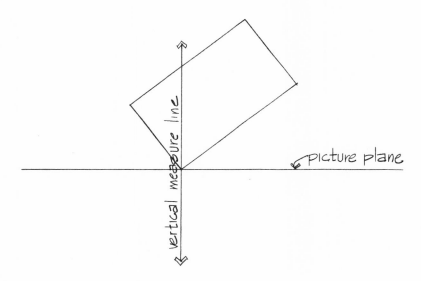

All vertical points in the drawing will be measured from this line at the same scale as the plan.

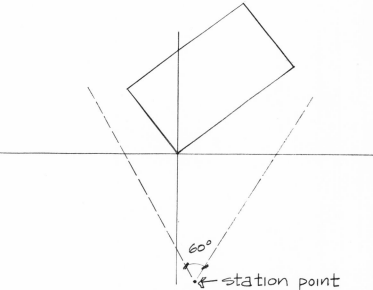

The station point can be further away but the drawing will tend to 'flatten' in perspective. If the station point is closer, the drawing will be distorted.

5. Draw the horizon line anywhere on the sheet. Determine the height of view for the drawing (bird's-eye view, human's eye view, etc.) and draw the ground line at that distance below the horizon line - same scale as plan.

6. To establish the vanishing points for two point perspective, draw two lines from the station point that are parallel to the sides of the plan.

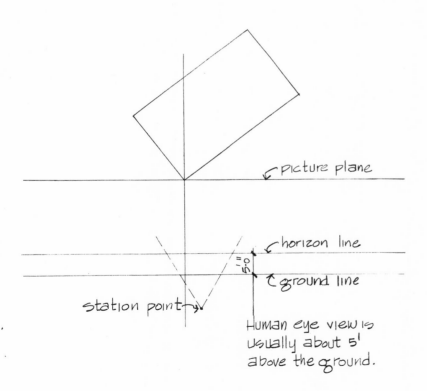

picture plane

horizon line

$\frac{1"}{5'0}$

ground line

station point

Human eye view is usually about 5' above the ground.

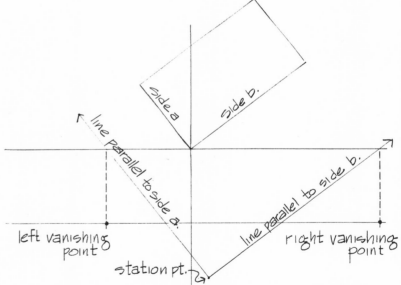

Side a

Side b.

line parallel to side a.

line parallel to side b.

left vanishing point

right vanishing point

station pt.

Where these lines cross the picture plane lines establishes the distance between the vanishing points. These points are then projected to the horizon line to establish the actual vanishing points.

PERSPECTIVE

7. Project a line from the station point (the viewer's eye) to each corner of the plan. Where this line crosses the picture plane is the location of that corner on your perspective drawing.

8. vertical measure is accurately scaled along the vertical measure line.

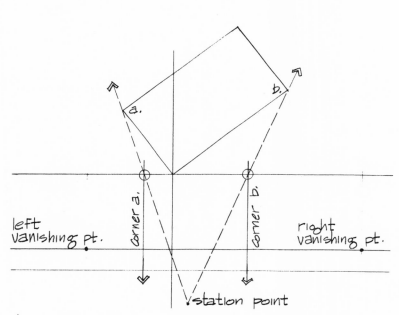

left vanishing pt.

corner a.

corner b.

right vanishing pt.

station point

Any other point on the plan can be located on the picture plane in a similar fashion.

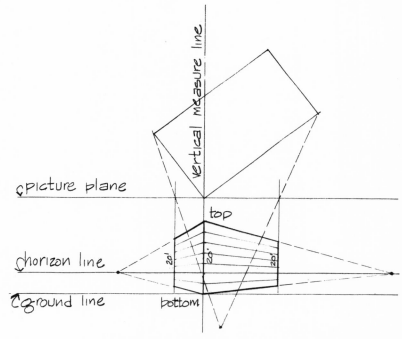

vertical measure line

picture plane

top

horizon line

20'   20'   20'

ground line   bottom

The top and bottom points are connected to the vanishing points at the corresponding sides of the drawing to determine the heights of similar corners behind the picture plane.

72

9. The corrected heights and locations of any point may be found in this manner, but some require a little more effort.

10. As we raise the horizon line above the ground plane, we raise the eye level of the viewer and begin to look down on the object (bird's-eye perspective)

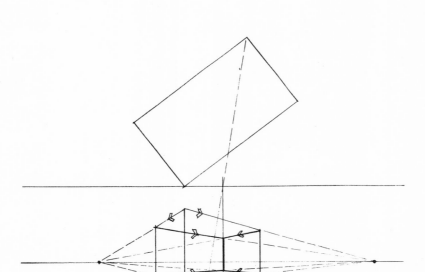

. station point

For example, to locate the back corner we must start at the vertical measure line and work our way around the various corners until we arrive at the proper spot.

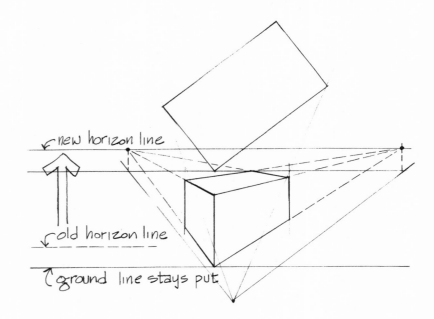

new horizon line

old horizon line

ground line stays put

PERSPECTIVE

THE EXAMPLE

More complex forms can be drawn with the same simple rules although some practice will be required to produce the drawings quickly. The small 'blocked out' drawing can then be enlarged on a xerox machine and rendered in detail.

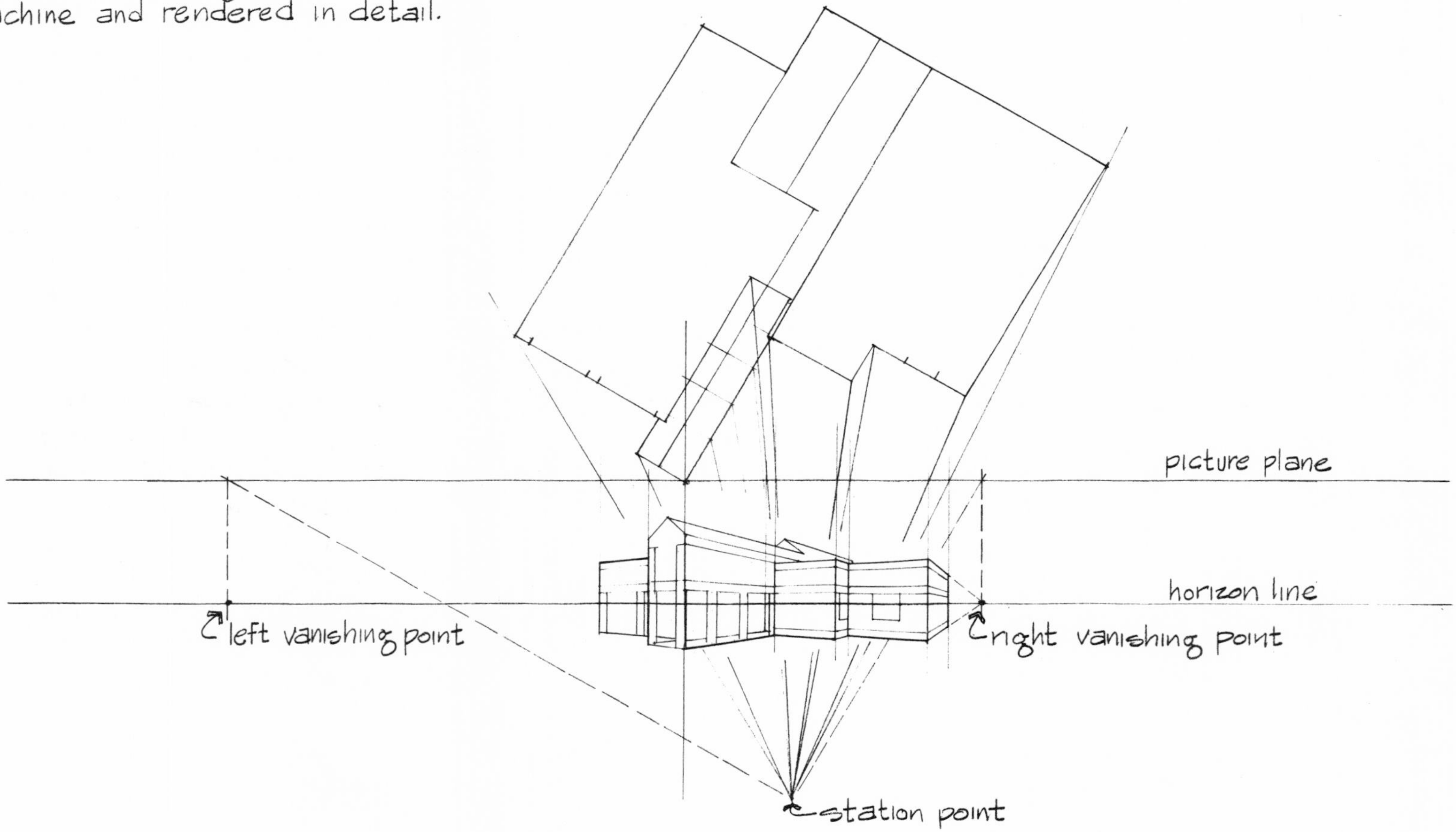
picture plane
horizon line
left vanishing point
right vanishing point
station point

CONSTRUCTION DOCUMENTS

Construction Documents, sometimes referred to as working drawings, are the actual plans and materials specifications which the contractor uses to price and build the building. They are technical to a degree and constitute a part of the legal contract or agreement between the owner and the contractor. If they are too sketchy and incomplete, the owner will have little control over the finished product and may wonder where his money was spent. This situation could also lead to expensive change orders as the construction materializes and the owner sees ways to add details or refine the original plan. The best way to avoid these pitfalls is to choose a contractor with a reputation for honesty and to have an architect or draftsperson draw the finished plans. If the major design decisions have been made during the previous exercises and they can be clearly conveyed to the drafts-person, the cost of actually producing the construction documents will be surprisingly low and well worth the price. The following chapter describes a "builder set" of documents which is concise and complete, but leaves most details to be constructed in the contractors preferred method.

CONSTRUCTION DOCUMENTS

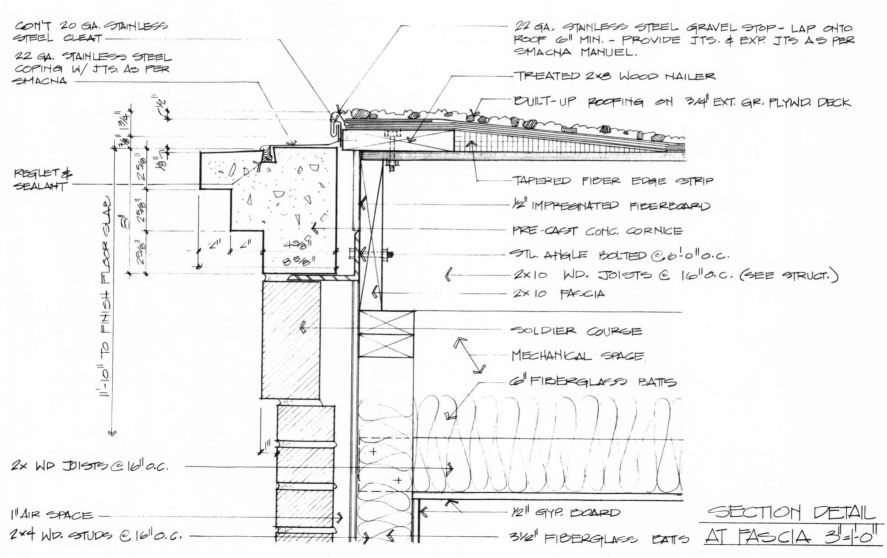

CON'T 20 GA. STAINLESS STEEL CLEAT

22 GA. STAINLESS STEEL COPING W/ JTS. AS PER SMACNA

REGLET & SEALANT

2x WD JOISTS @ 16" O.C.

1" AIR SPACE

2x4 WD. STUDS @ 16" O.C.

11'-0" TO FINISH FLOOR SLAB

22 GA. STAINLESS STEEL GRAVEL STOP - LAP ONTO ROOF 6" MIN. - PROVIDE JTS. & EXP. JTS AS PER SMACNA MANUEL.

TREATED 2x8 WOOD NAILER

BUILT-UP ROOFING ON 3/4" EXT. GR. PLYWD. DECK

TAPERED FIBER EDGE STRIP

1/2" IMPREGNATED FIBERBOARD

PRE-CAST CONC. CORNICE

STL. ANGLE BOLTED @ 6'-0" O.C.

2x10 WD. JOISTS @ 16" O.C. (SEE STRUCT.)

2x10 FASCIA

SOLDIER COURSE

MECHANICAL SPACE

6" FIBERGLASS BATTS

1/2" GYP. BOARD

3 1/2" FIBERGLASS BATTS

SECTION DETAIL
AT FASCIA 3"=1'-0"

CONSTRUCTION DOCUMENTS

All cities and townships and some counties require the issuance of a building permit before you can begin construction. You or your contractor must submit enough drawings to give the building inspector a reasonable idea of the proposed structure and its materials. This process assures a certain quality minimum and protects neighborhoods and future purchasers.

The Building Inspector will provide you with a list of the required drawings and scales. It usually contains the following:

Site Plan	1/8, 1/10, or 1/20 scale
Foundation Plan	1/8 or 1/4
Floor Plan	1/8 or 1/4
Minimum 2 Elevations	1/8 or 1/4
Typical Building Section	1/8 or 1/4
Typical Wall Section	1/2 or 3/4
Roof Framing Plan	1/8 or 1/4
Outline Specifications	written

CONSTRUCTION DOCUMENTS

SITE PLAN

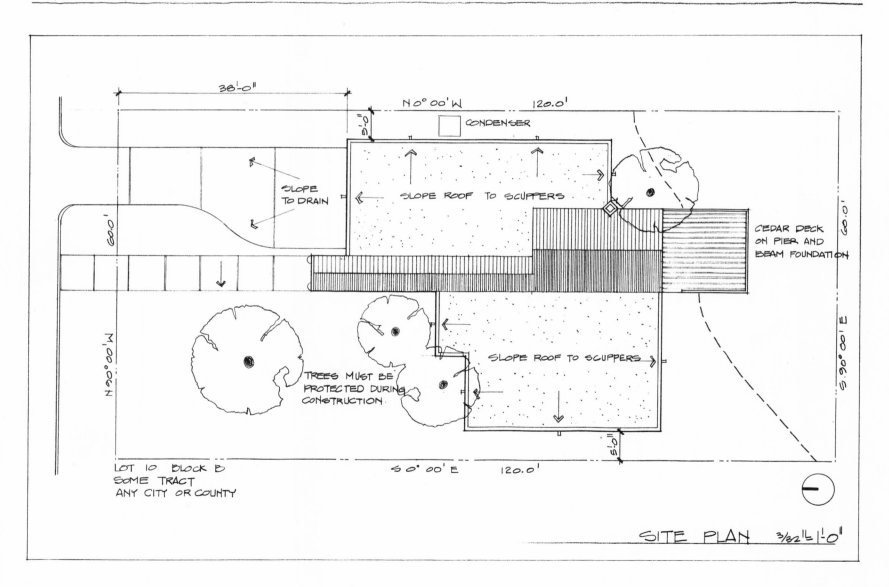

38'-0"

N 0° 00' W   120.0'

5'-0"

□ CONDENSER

SLOPE
TO DRAIN

SLOPE ROOF TO SCUPPERS

60.0'

CEDAR DECK
ON PIER AND
BEAM FOUNDATION

60.0'

N 90° 00' W

S 90° 00' E

TREES MUST BE
PROTECTED DURING
CONSTRUCTION

SLOPE ROOF TO SCUPPERS

5'-0"

LOT 10 BLOCK B
SOME TRACT
ANY CITY OR COUNTY

S 0° 00' E   120.0'

SITE PLAN 3/32"=1'-0"

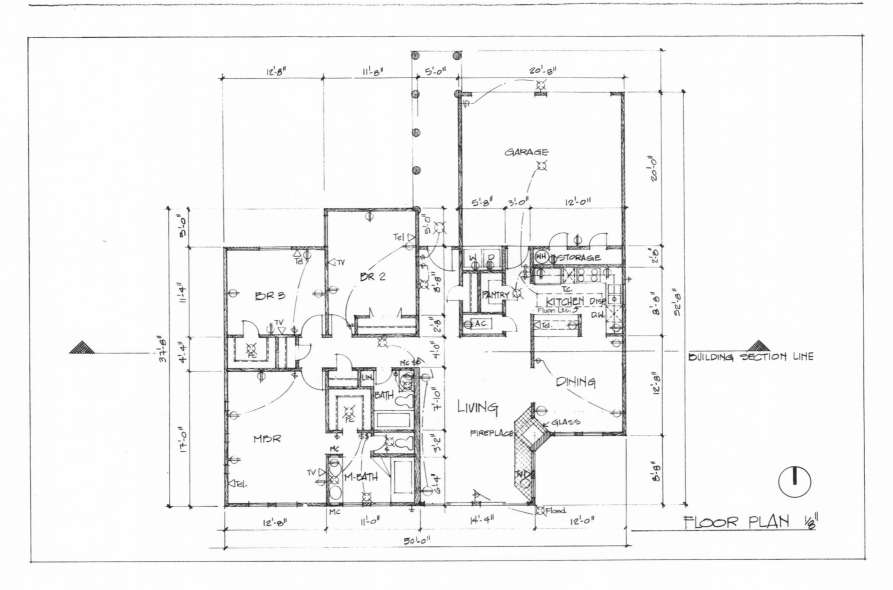

BUILDING SECTION LINE

FLOOR PLAN ⅛"

CONSTRUCTION DOCUMENTS

ELEVATIONS

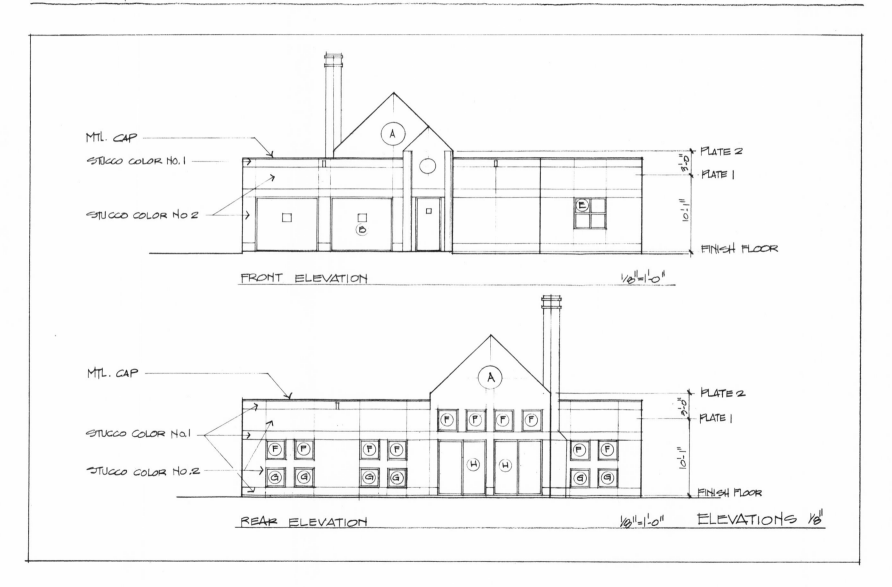

MTL. CAP

STUCCO COLOR NO. 1

STUCCO COLOR NO 2

PLATE 2

PLATE 1

FINISH FLOOR

FRONT ELEVATION

1/8" = 1'-0"

MTL. CAP

STUCCO COLOR No. 1

STUCCO COLOR No. 2

PLATE 2

PLATE 1

FINISH FLOOR

REAR ELEVATION

1/8" = 1'-0"

ELEVATIONS 1/8"

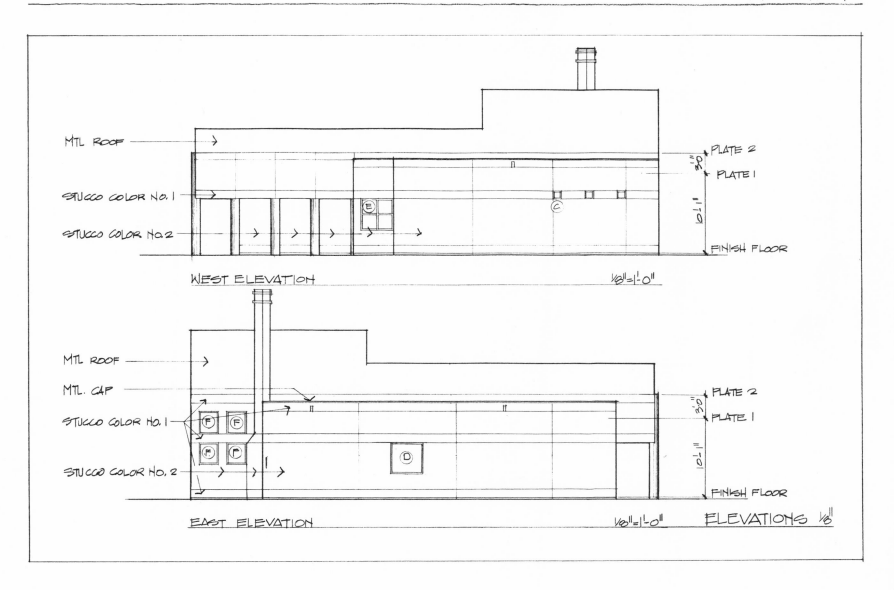

MTL ROOF

STUCCO COLOR No. 1

STUCCO COLOR No. 2

PLATE 2

PLATE 1

3'-0"

10'-1"

FINISH FLOOR

WEST ELEVATION   1/8"=1'-0"

MTL ROOF

MTL. CAP

STUCCO COLOR No. 1

STUCCO COLOR No. 2

PLATE 2

PLATE 1

3'-0"

10'-1"

FINISH FLOOR

EAST ELEVATION   1/8"=1'-0"   ELEVATIONS 1/8"

CONSTRUCTION DOCUMENTS

SECTION

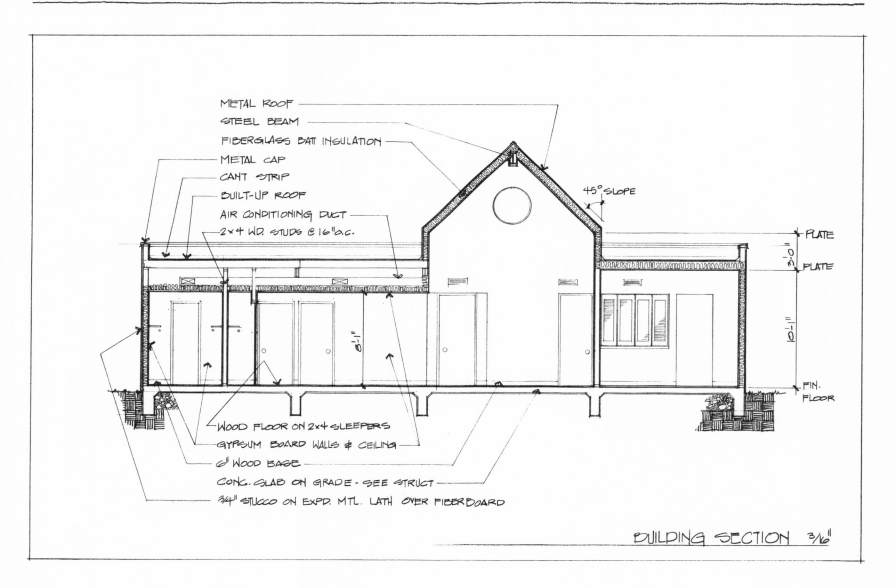

METAL ROOF

STEEL BEAM

FIBERGLASS BATT INSULATION

METAL CAP

CANT STRIP

BUILT-UP ROOF

AIR CONDITIONING DUCT

2×4 WD. STUDS @ 16" O.C.

45° SLOPE

PLATE

PLATE

FIN. FLOOR

WOOD FLOOR ON 2×4 SLEEPERS

GYPSUM BOARD WALLS & CEILING

6" WOOD BASE

CONC. SLAB ON GRADE - SEE STRUCT

3/4" STUCCO ON EXPD. MTL. LATH OVER FIBERBOARD

BUILDING SECTION 3/16"

82

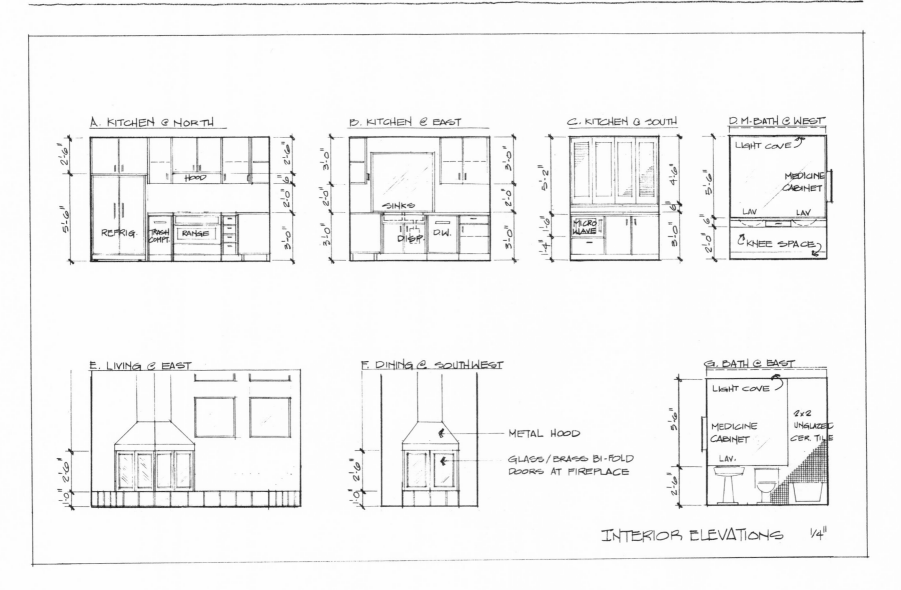

A. KITCHEN @ NORTH

HOOD

REFRIG. | TRASH COMPT. | RANGE

B. KITCHEN @ EAST

SINKS

DISP. | D.W.

C. KITCHEN @ SOUTH

MICRO WAVE

D. M-BATH @ WEST

LIGHT COVE

MEDICINE CABINET

LAV | LAV

KNEE SPACE

E. LIVING @ EAST

F. DINING @ SOUTHWEST

— METAL HOOD

— GLASS/BRASS BI-FOLD DOORS AT FIREPLACE

G. BATH @ EAST

LIGHT COVE

MEDICINE CABINET

LAV.

2x2 UNGLAZED CER. TILE

INTERIOR ELEVATIONS   1/4"

CONSTRUCTION DOCUMENTS

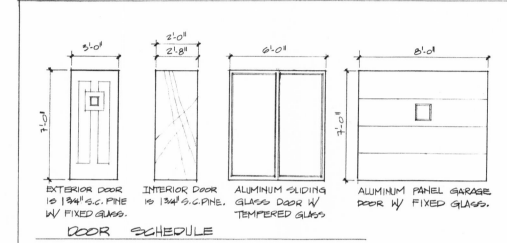

EXTERIOR DOOR IS 1¾" S.C. PINE W/ FIXED GLASS.

INTERIOR DOOR IS 1¾" S.C. PINE.

ALUMINUM SLIDING GLASS DOOR W/ TEMPERED GLASS

ALUMINUM PANEL GARAGE DOOR W/ FIXED GLASS.

DOOR SCHEDULE

WINDOW SCHEDULE

WINDOW	MANUFACTURER	TYPE
A	CONTRACTOR	FIXED ¼" PLATE
B		
C		
D		
E	ANY COMPANY	DOUBLE HUNG ALUM.
F	CONTRACTOR	FIXED ¼" PLATE
G	ANY COMPANY	AWNING -ALUM.

ROOM FINISH SCHEDULE

ITEM ROOM	FLOOR	BASE	CEILING MATERIAL	CEILING HEIGHT	WALLS NORTH	WALLS SOUTH	WALLS EAST	WALLS WEST	OTHER
GARAGE	CONC.	4" WD.	GYP. BRD.	10'-0"	GYP. BRD.	GYP. BRD.	GYP. BRD.	GYP. BRD.	
ENTRY	WOOD	6" WD.	"	8'-0"	"	"	"	"	
KITCHEN	TILE	"	"	10'-0"	"	"	"	"	
DINING	WOOD	"	"	"	"	"	"	"	
LIVING	"	"	"	SLOPED	"	"	"	"	TILE @ HEARTH
BATH	TILE	TILE	"	8'-0"	TILE	TILE	TILE	TILE	¼" PLATE MIRROR
M-BATH	"	"	"	"	"	"	"	"	"
MBR	WOOD	6" WD.	"	10'-0"	GYP. BRD.	GYP. BRD	GYP. BRD	GYP. BRD.	
BR 2	"	"	"	"	"	"	"	"	
BR 3	"	"	"	"	"	"	"	"	
CORRIDOR	"	"	"	8'-0"	"	"	"	"	
CLOSETS	"	"	"	"	"	"	"	"	

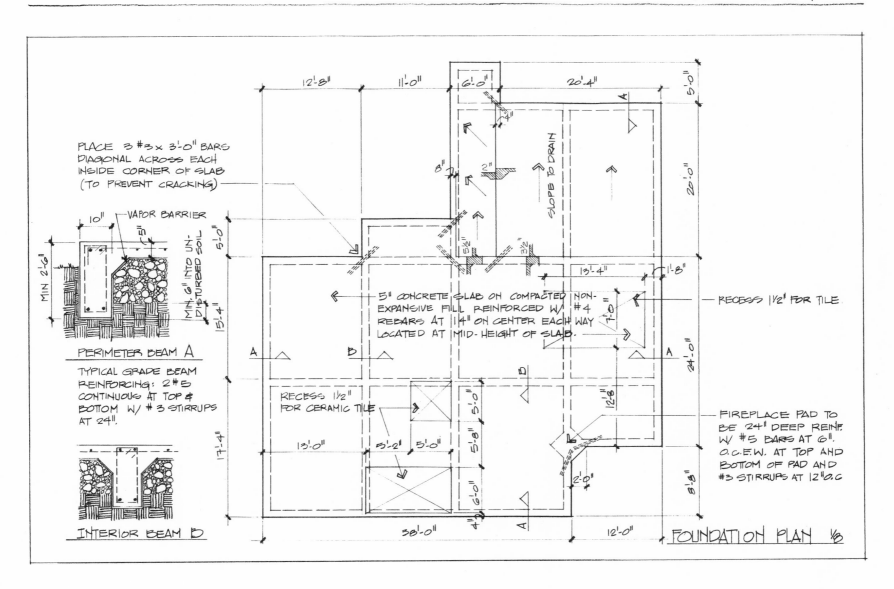

PLACE 3 #3 x 3'-0" BARS DIAGONAL ACROSS EACH INSIDE CORNER OF SLAB (TO PREVENT CRACKING)

VAPOR BARRIER

PERIMETER BEAM A

TYPICAL GRADE BEAM REINFORCING: 2 #5 CONTINUOUS AT TOP & BOTTOM W/ #3 STIRRUPS AT 24".

INTERIOR BEAM B

SLOPE TO DRAIN

5" CONCRETE SLAB ON COMPACTED NON-EXPANSIVE FILL REINFORCED W/ #4 REBARS AT 14" ON CENTER EACH WAY LOCATED AT MID-HEIGHT OF SLAB.

RECESS 1½" FOR CERAMIC TILE

RECESS 1½" FOR TILE

FIREPLACE PAD TO BE 24" DEEP REINF. W/ #5 BARS AT 6". O.C.E.W. AT TOP AND BOTTOM OF PAD AND #3 STIRRUPS AT 12" O.C

FOUNDATION PLAN ⅛

CONSTRUCTION DOCUMENTS

ROOF FRAMING PLAN

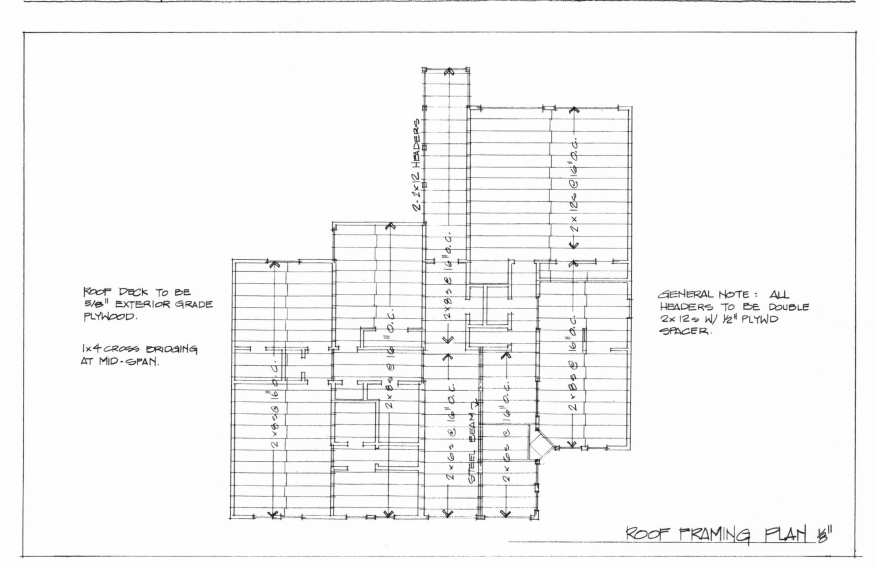

ROOF DECK TO BE
5/8" EXTERIOR GRADE
PLYWOOD.

1×4 CROSS BRIDGING
AT MID-SPAN.

GENERAL NOTE: ALL
HEADERS TO BE DOUBLE
2×12s W/ ½" PLYWD
SPACER.

ROOF FRAMING PLAN ⅛"

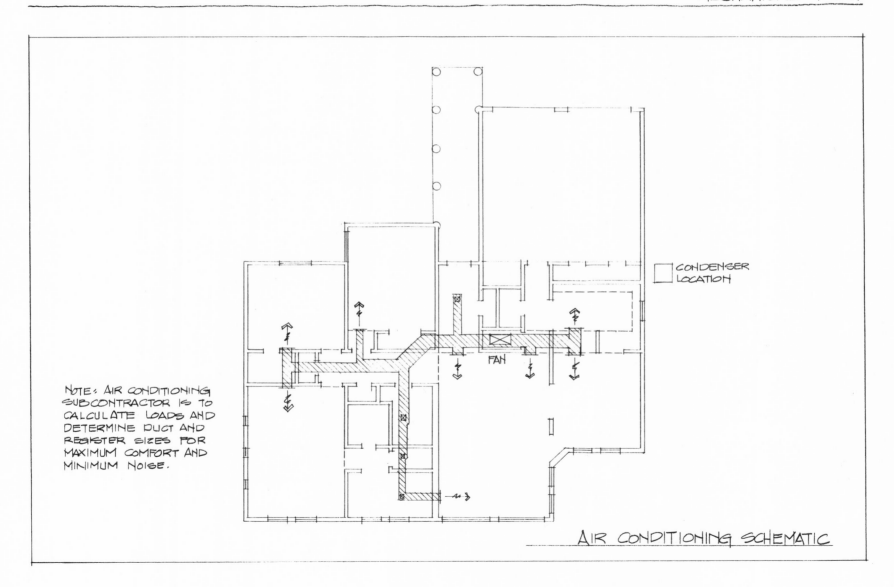

NOTE: AIR CONDITIONING
SUBCONTRACTOR IS TO
CALCULATE LOADS AND
DETERMINE DUCT AND
REGISTER SIZES FOR
MAXIMUM COMFORT AND
MINIMUM NOISE.

CONDENSER
LOCATION

FAN

AIR CONDITIONING SCHEMATIC

CONSTRUCTION DOCUMENTS

OUTLINE SPECIFICATIONS

FOUNDATION: 5" CONCRETE SLAB ON GRADE. MIN. 5 SACKS PER CUBIC YARD, 6" SLUMP. MAX. 6 GALLONS WATER PER SACK. CONCRETE SHALL BE 3000 P.S.I, STEEL SHALL BE 40,000 P.S.I. WATERPROOFING SHALL BE .006" PLASTIC MEMBRANE. SEE STRUCTURAL FOR PLANS AND DETAILS.

FIREPLACE: CUSTOM DESIGN - SEE PLANS AND INTERIOR ELEVATIONS FOR DETAILS, CONTRACTOR MUST SUBMIT SHOP DRAWINGS TO OWNER.

EXTERIOR WALLS: WOOD FRAME SHALL BE KILN DRIED STANDARD OR BETTER FIR OR #2 YELLOW PINE, 2×4 AT 16" ON CENTER, WITH CORNER BRACING. SHEATHING IS ½" IMPREGNATED FIBERBOARD. EXTERIOR FINISH IS ¾" STUCCO IN 3 COATS ON EXPANDED METAL LATH WITH CORNER BEADS AND CONTROL JOINTS. COLOR WILL BE SELECTED BY OWNER. EXTERIOR PAINT WILL BE EXTERIOR GRADE LATEX.

ROOF FRAMING: JOISTS, BEAMS AND RAFTERS SHALL BE KILN DRIED STANDARD OR BETTER FIR OR #2 YELLOW PINE WITH 1×4 CROSS BRIDGING. ROOF DECK WILL BE ⅝" C-C PLUGGED EXTERIOR GRADE PLYWOOD.

ROOFING: METAL ROOF SHALL BE ALUMINUM INTER-LOCKING STANDING SEAM INDUSTRIAL SYSTEM. BUILT-UP ROOF WILL BE 4-PLY 20 YEAR HOT MOP PROCESS W/ 28 GA. G.I. FLASHING.

FINISH FLOORING: WOOD FLOORING WILL BE ¾" × 2" TONGUE AND GROOVE OAK FLOORING ON WOOD SLEEPERS. KITCHEN TILE IS ¾"×12"×12" MEXICAN SAND TILE, THICK SET. BATH TILE IS 2×2 UNGLAZED CERAMIC TILE.

DOORS: INTERIOR DOORS TO BE 1¾" SOLID CORE PINE W/ CUSTOM TRIM.

EXTERIOR DOORS TO BE 1¾" S.C. PINE.

SLIDING GLASS DOORS ARE ALUMINUM W/ TEMPERED SINGLE GLAZED GLASS.

WINDOWS: OPERABLE WINDOWS SHALL BE SINGLE GLAZED ALUMINUM UNITS.

FIXED GLASS UNITS SHALL BE ¼" PLATE W/ WOOD STOPS.

MIRRORS ARE ¼" PLATE.

CABINETS: CABINETS SHALL BE ¾" R.C. BIRCH, PAINTED, COUNTERTOPS ARE PLASTIC LAMINATE W/ 1×2 OAK TRIM.

MEDICINE CABINETS ARE PRE-FAB UNITS WITH ADJUSTABLE GLASS SHELVES AND WOOD LOUVERED DOOR.

PLUMBING: OWNER WILL SELECT FIXTURES FROM ALLOWANCE.

WATER SUPPLY AND SEWAGE DISPOSAL ARE PUBLIC SYSTEMS.

HOUSE DRAIN SHALL BE CAST IRON.

WATER PIPING SHALL BE COPPER TUBING.

WATER HEATER SHALL BE 52 GALLON, TEN YEAR GAS FIRED W/ FIBERGLASS TANK

GAS PROVIDED BY UTILITY COMPANY

CONTINUED

ELECTRICAL: SERVICE SHALL BE UNDERGROUND WITH CIRCUIT BREAKER.

WIRING SHALL BE COPPER WITH SPECIAL OUTLETS FOR RANGE, WATER HEATER, DISHWASHER, TRASH COMPACTER, WASHER, DRYER, REFRIGERATOR, MICRO-WAVE OVEN.

LIGHTING FIXTURES WILL BE SELECTED BY OWNER WITHIN ALLOWANCE.

MECHANICAL: HEATING/AIR CONDITIONING SYSTEM WILL BE A FORCED AIR CENTRAL UNIT WITH OVERHEAD DUCT SUPPLY. SUB CONTRACTOR WILL SUBMIT DRAWINGS FOR APPROVAL.

MECHANICAL VENTS AT RESTROOMS.

INSULATION: 6" FIBERGLASS BATTS IN ROOF & CEILING.

3½" FIBERGLASS BATTS IN WALLS.

HARDWARE: OWNER WILL SELECT HARDWARE FROM ALLOWANCE.

EQUIPMENT: OWNER WILL SELECT EQUIPMENT FROM ALLOWANCE.

WALKS & DRIVES: SHALL BE 4" CONCRETE SLAB ON GRADE REINFORCED W/ #4 BARS AT 14" O.C.E.W.

LANDSCAPING: BY OWNER

CLEAN-UP: BY CONTRACTOR

CONSTRUCTION DOCUMENTS

REPRODUCTION METHODS

During and after the drawing process, inexpensive copies of original drawings must be made for overlay, to give to the building inspector, the contractor, subcontractors, bank, etc. The standard is the blueline print which can be made at any architectural printing company. Reproduction methods are explained below.

Blueline Prints - A diazo/ammonia process by which a light passes through the translucent vellum drawings and exposes a coated paper, which is then developed. Inexpensive and fast process for full size drawings.

2080 Xerox - This is a xerox process that can reduce or enlarge original drawings on vellum or less expensive bond paper. An added advantage is that copies can be made from opaque originals onto vellum and then blueline prints made from that copy.

Regular Xerox - Most xerox machines will reproduce sizes up to 11" x 17". This will not be large enough for most house plans but it is very inexpensive and a useful tool for copying details, etc. during the drawing process. Full scale plans can be reduced on the 2080 xerox to 11" x 17" size and then be reproduced cheaply by regular xerox for bidding purposes, etc.

Blueprints - This is a similar process to blue-line prints, except the negative. It is seldom used these days.

TRANSFORMER

This chapter deals with the importance of planning ahead, especially when one is building on a limited budget. Future expansion must be considered in the initial phase in order not to design oneself into the proverbial corner. Financial alternatives such as the use of a portion of the house for a temporary office or apartment can also be considered at this time. In any scenario of the future, the design with the most adaptibility will have the best chance of economic survival.

The following example is also an exercise in designing a house to work on any site. A careful study of the plan should give the reader a good feeling for these issues and those of multi-story house design.

TRANSFORMER

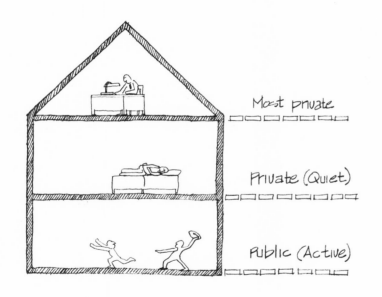

Most private

Private (Quiet)

Public (Active)

A multi-story house can be designed by the same methods as a single story, but it is slightly more complicated. Vertical circulation must be worked out between the floors, head room at vertical circulation as well as any attic rooms must be verified in sections, structural integrity must be maintained through each level, and vertical mechanical (air and plumbing risers) must be coordinated. The following example will work through the multi-level design process. The goal of this design will be to produce a highly efficient well-designed plan with maximum interior flexibility and site adaptability at a minimum cost.

Zoning in a multi-level house may have a vertical separation between private and public areas, usually with more active areas located on lowest levels.

This house is called 'the Transformer' because it can change as the owner's needs change. It is designed for maximum space efficiency, flexibility, finance-ability, site-adaptability, and expansion. This type of careful long-range planning will allow the owner to build only what he/she needs at the time of initial construction, greatly reducing the amount of initial financing and therefore lower payments. It begins as a 1 bedroom, 1½ bath with study and can transform in a very cost efficient fashion into a 5 bedroom + study, 3½ bath house.

For maximum site adaptability, the house width is set at 25', which will work on a townhouse lot or on any size single family lot with ample allowance for natural features and orientation.

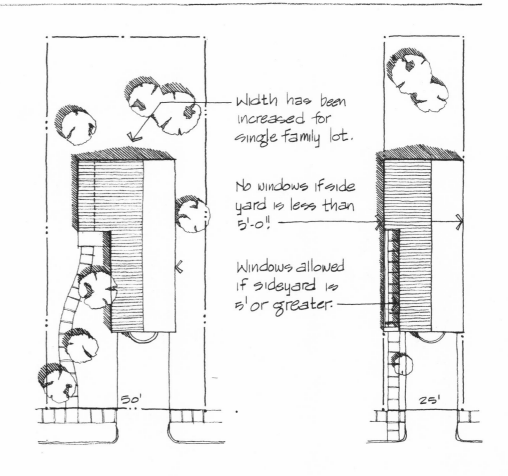

Width has been increased for single family lot.

No windows if side yard is less than 5'-0"

Windows allowed if sideyard is 5' or greater.

50'

25'

Site Plan for Average Lot   Townhouse Lot

TRANSFORMER

For initial budget reasons, we will limit the program to a one bedroom house with a studio and 1½ baths. Plumbing for future expansion will be installed at this time.

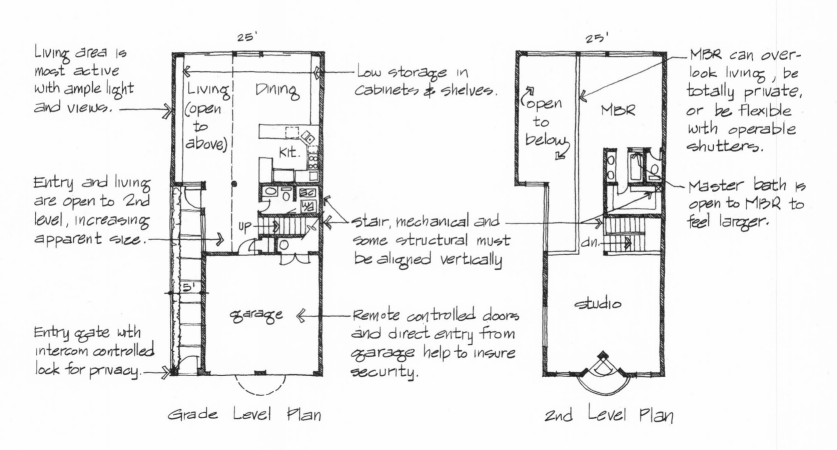

Living area is most active with ample light and views.

Entry and living are open to 2nd level, increasing apparent size.

Entry gate with intercom controlled lock for privacy.

25'

Living (open to above)

Dining

Kit.

UP

garage

5'

Grade Level Plan

Low storage in cabinets & shelves.

stair, mechanical and some structural must be aligned vertically

Remote controlled doors and direct entry from garage help to insure security.

25'

open to below

MBR

studio

dn.

2nd Level Plan

MBR can overlook living, be totally private, or be flexible with operable shutters.

Master bath is open to MBR to feel larger.

This transformation allows the studio to become either a self-contained office or efficiency apartment with its own entry and total privacy from the house proper. Either of these transformations can help defray initial payment burden.

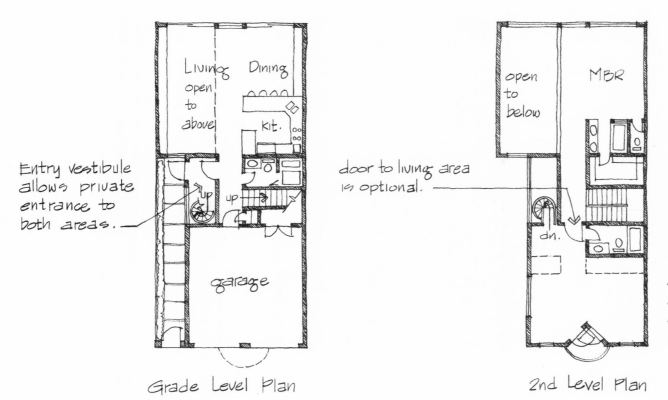

Entry vestibule allows private entrance to both areas.

door to living area is optional.

Bath addition makes studio into a self-contained tax deductable office. Kitchenette and closet make an income generating apartment.

Grade Level Plan

2nd Level Plan

TRANSFORMER

In order to secure financing, the lending institution must be convinced that the house has a good resale potential, which usually translates into 3 bedrooms and 2½ baths.

This transformation can be accomplished by the addition of the extra bath and a few walls. Most institutions will finance a 'singles' house if it can be easily converted.

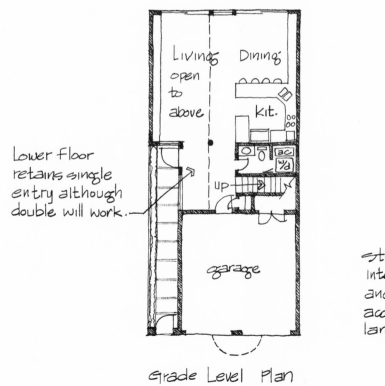

Living
open to above

Dining

kit.

UP

Lower floor retains single entry although double will work.

garage

Grade Level Plan

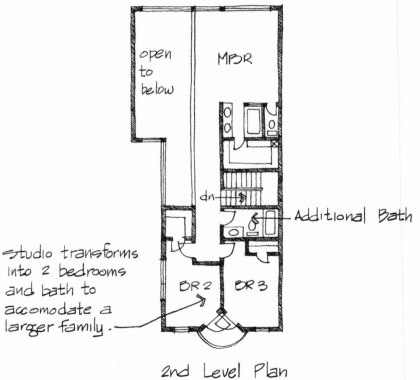

open to below

MBR

dn

Additional Bath

studio transforms into 2 bedrooms and bath to accomodate a larger family.

BR 2   BR 3

2nd Level Plan

The simple addition of another stair level transforms attic space into another group of bedrooms or study. This area should also have a
skylight or some equivalent means of easy egress
in case a fire might block the stair.

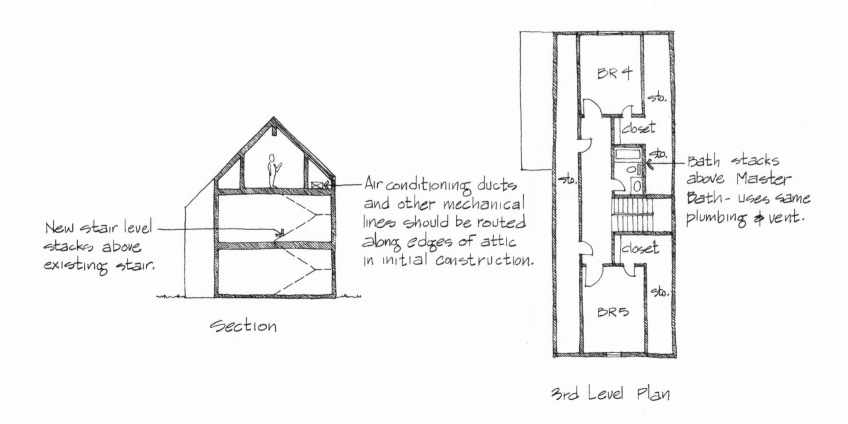

New stair level
stacks above
existing stair.

Section

Air conditioning ducts
and other mechanical
lines should be routed
along edges of attic
in initial construction.

BR 4

sto.

closet

sto.

sto.

Bath stacks
above Master
Bath- uses same
plumbing & vent.

closet

sto.

BR 5

3rd Level Plan

97

TRANSFORMER

The last built-in expansion possibility would be to frame in all or part of the space above the living area for a nursery or a study/sewing room. Again this can be easily accomplished because we have planned ahead not only in architectural concerns but also in structural and mechanical systems.

The total amount of dollars for this built-in flexibility has been a very small part of our initial construction price but it has allowed us to add on in an efficient manner when and where we needed the space.

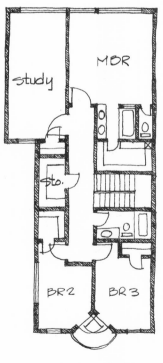

2nd Level Plan

There are as many possibilities for an elevation as there are bedrooms, but here is one way it might look. We will save money by providing exterior openings for future spaces in the initial construction and also have a more interesting facade.

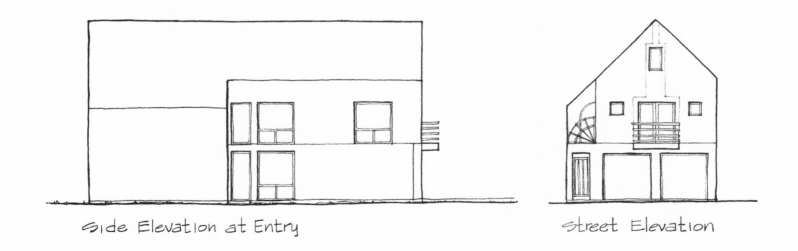

Side Elevation at Entry   Street Elevation

TRANSFORMER

Another slight modification can transform this house into the super energy efficient solar envelope concept. All we need do is add the solar greenhouse to the south (entry) elevation, raise the structure slightly, and provide a double wall at the north elevation for air flow. See appendix for more detailed information on this concept.

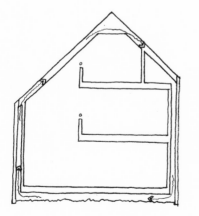

Open upper levels can assist in a natural ventilation concept - see appendix.

Section at Living Area

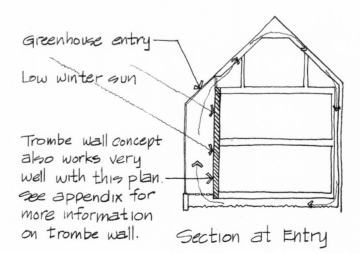

Greenhouse entry

Low winter sun

Trombe wall concept also works very well with this plan. See appendix for more information on trombe wall.

Section at Entry

MATERIALS

A good designer will be thinking about building materials all the way through the design process. Many types of materials will accomplish the same end at considerable cost differences. Some materials lend themselves to certain shapes and massing configurations and others have strong emotional implications. Almost all materials come in stock modular sizes which can be utilized by a designer to eliminate much waste and labor. Value engineering looks for alternate materials with better value; either in front-end cost, expected life, or maintenance costs. For example, some extra material cost may be off-set by favorable insurance premiums for using that material. This chapter presents some typical residential materials along with price comparisons and other relative information to provide the reader with some background for material selection.

MATERIALS

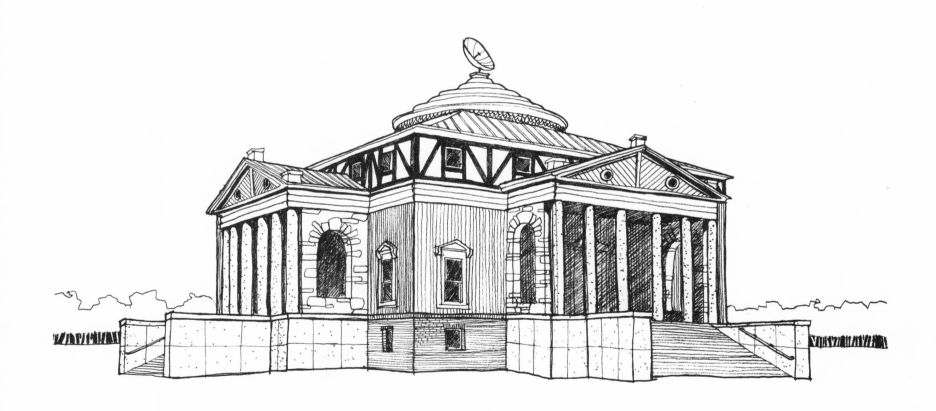

Too many different materials can confound even the most classical designs.

Once you have arrived at the plan that complements your lifestyle, a contractor will be happy to provide you with a cost estimate which can itemize different systems costs and alternates for that plan. Then you can easily compare the emotional value of certain materials and details to the dollar value of their substitutes.

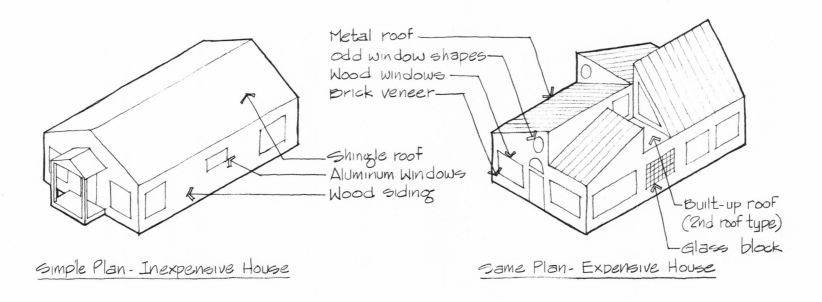

Metal roof
odd window shapes
Wood windows
Brick veneer

Shingle roof
Aluminum Windows
Wood siding

Built-up roof
(2nd roof type)
Glass block

Simple Plan - Inexpensive House

Same Plan - Expensive House

Of course the more information a contractor has in the way of drawings and models, the more accurate the price he delivers.

MATERIALS

SHEATHING MATERIALS

This chapter is devoted to some basic types of building materials and their available sizes and comparative prices. If we can select the materials before we begin design we can maximize the amount of house for the money. By designing to the modular size of the material we can eliminate much of the waste.

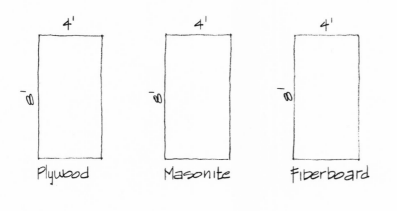

Plywood   Masonite   Fiberboard

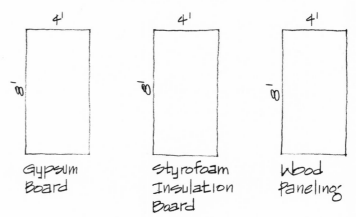

Gypsum Board   Styrofoam Insulation Board   Wood Paneling

In North America, most sheathing materials are based on a 4 foot by 8' foot modular size. Lumber is available in 2 foot increments of even numbered feet plus about 1½" (i.e. 8'-1½", 10'-1½", 12'-1½"). This length plus the plate thicknesses allow the studs to be trimmed slightly and maintain a total wall height of 8'-1". The full 8' sheathing can then be placed on the wall without a cut. The base trim makes up the difference.

WOOD

Inexpensive front end cost but some amount
of maintenance will be required.

T-III

T-III (pronounced Tee-one-eleven) plywood is an
exterior grade of plywood with grooves in the
outer layer to simulate vertical slat siding. Top
horizontal edge must be protected from water
with a strip of pre-molded metal flashing. This
siding provides a skin diaphragm which acts as
diagonal bracing for the building.
Sizes are 4'x8' x 1/4", 3/8", 1/2", 5/8", 3/4"
Price for 5/8" exterior grade about $1.26 psf.

MASONITE

Masonite Exterior siding is similar to T-III plywood in appearance and price but is made of
pressed wood fibers and glue. It also comes
in many textures
Sizes are 4'x8', 4'x9', 4'x10', 12"x16'
Price for 3/8" exterior grade about $1.24 psf.

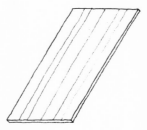 

MATERIALS

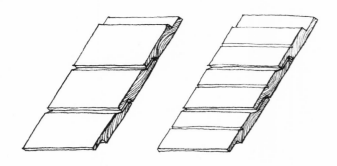

WOOD SIDING

Wood slat siding is cut from solid pieces of sawn lumber, 3/4" thick, which overlap one another for water protection. There is no possibility of delamination but the siding itself does not furnish adequate diagonal bracing. Price is about $1.00 per square foot in place.

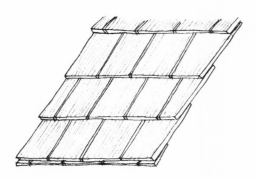

WOOD SHINGLES

Wood singles can be split or sawn. They are lapped on the wall just as in roof construction. It is a very flexible material for tight radius curves and free forms. They are usually of cedar and require no painting and little maintenance. Price is about 90¢ per square foot installed.

MATERIALS

STUCCO

Stucco is a flexible exterior skin built up of
layers of cement plaster over expanded metal
laths. It can be colored and painted, requires
little or no maintenance, is fireproof, and can
turn corners and curves easily. It is available
in many textures. Price is about $2.80 per
square foot in place.

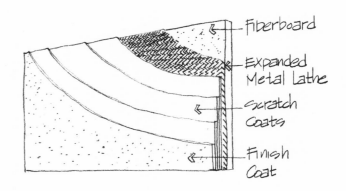

DRY-VIT

Dry-vit resembles stucco from a distance but it
is actually a very thin layer of cement plaster
applied over a fiberglass lath stretched over
a sandwich of 1" insulation board laminated
to 1/2" gypsum board. It is available in more
colors than stucco and is color-fast. Many
intricate styrofoam forms and moldings are
fabricated to be used with this system. The
major drawback is its vulnerability to damage
from vandals or automobiles. Price is about
$5.00 per square foot installed.

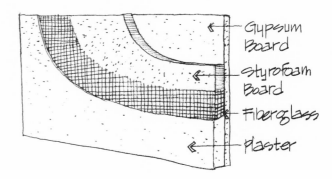

MATERIALS

BRICK

Brick is a molded clay product fired in kilns for hardening. It comes in a few standard shapes and sizes and a wide variety of colors. It lends a sense of solidity and stability to a residence (re: three little pigs) and is fireproof. It can be detailed in many ways to create a very interesting and refined exterior skin. Main sizes are 3"x8", 3"x9", & 3"x10". Installed cost is about $6.50 per square foot.

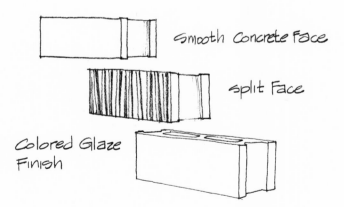

Smooth Concrete Face

Split Face

Colored Glaze Finish

CONCRETE BLOCK

Concrete Block is a modular concrete product available in a wide variety of textures, finishes, and sizes. It is larger than a brick which reduces labor costs but it tends to have an industrial connotation. Typical sizes are 4"x 8"x16", 6"x8"x 16", 8"x8"x16", up to 12" deep. Cost in place is about $4.00 per square foot.

MATERIALS

STONE

Natural stone can make a particularly handsome
exterior wall surface, however, it is expensive.
Each stone must be custom cut and fitted into
the wall. Installed price is about $16.00 per
square foot and up, depending on the stone.

METAL

Corrugated Iron or Aluminum can also make an
attractive exterior wall in the industrial
style of grain elevators or barns. It is easy
to work and requires little maintenance. It is
usually employed with a steel structural
system but can be easily adapted to custom
wood stud framing. It also works well as
a roofing material. Price in place is about
$2.00 per square foot.

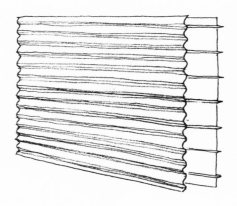

MATERIALS

GYP. BOARD

Gypsum board is by far the most versatile and popular interior wall and ceiling finish material. It is very inexpensive, easy to work, and the joints can be hidden with tape and plaster. It is usually painted but it can also be papered or covered with vinyl. Sizes are 4 x 8

WOOD PANELING

Wood paneling comes in a broad range of price and quality and it is easy to install and very popular, especially among families with small children (it can be cleaned easily). Horizontal joints must be covered with a small trim piece. The wood grain and color can be considered either homey and secure or dark and oppressive. Sizes are 4 x 8

MATERIALS

VINYL COMPOSITION TILES

Vinyl tiles are very thin squares of vinyl that are applied to the subfloor with a mastic adhesive. They come in a variety of colors and are very easy to install. More interesting floors can be had by using color patterns or borders. Very low maintenance. Standard size is 12" x 12". Cost in place is about $ 1.80 per square foot.

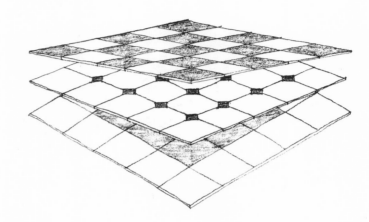

ROLL VINYL

Roll vinyl also comes in many patterns and colors. It has the same characteristics as vinyl squares. but is quicker to put down. Seams can be successfully hidden. Roll widths are typically 6'and 12'. Installed price is about $1.50 per square foot.

MATERIALS

FLOOR

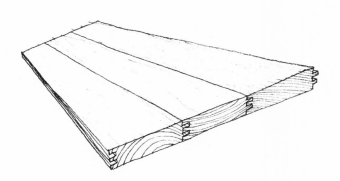

WOOD

Tongue and groove wood is still the most popular floor among architects for its warmth and emotion. It can be stained to any desirable shade of lightness or darkness and/or sealed with any gloss desirable for just the right look. Area rugs can be used to soften the room and define spaces. Even some softer, less expensive woods can be used quite successfully.

wood	size	price/sf in place
pine	1" x 4"	$2.45
oak	25/32" x 2 1/4"	$3.35
maple	25/32" x 2 1/4"	$3.30

CARPET

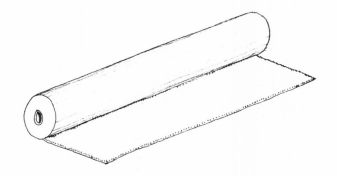

Carpet can be a very inexpensive way to provide that quality floor feeling. It can be applied directly over plywood sub-flooring or concrete slab, or over a pad for extra plush. Many commercial grades are available in beautiful piles at low cost. Installed price as low as $10 - $12 per square yard or $1.30 per square foot.

CONCRETE

Concrete can become a very pleasant and inexpensive floor. It can be painted or stained and polished. It can also be patterned with saw cuts or stamped to resemble various tile patterns. Cost is about $4.00 per square foot.

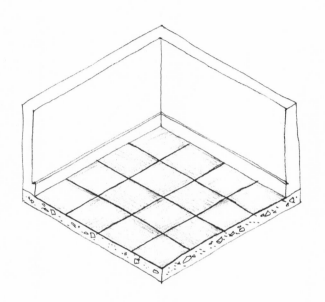

CERAMIC TILES

Ceramic tiles are thin pavers molded from clay and fired very hot which gives them an extreme hardness. They can be glazed or plain and come in a wide variety of patterns, colors, finishes, and sizes. They can be 'thin set' or laid into a cement bed and grouted. Typical sizes are 4" x 8" up to 12" x 12". Cost in place is about $4.00 per square foot.

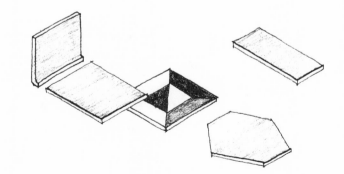

MATERIALS

ASPHALT SHINGLES

Asphalt shingles are still the least expensive, good looking roof money can buy. They come in a variety of colors and can be applied directly over older shingles. They are non-combustable and cost about 90¢ per square foot in place.

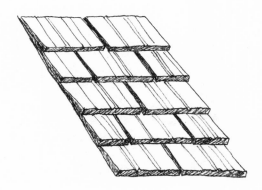

WOOD SHINGLES

Hand split wood 'shakes' or sawn wood shingles are a beautiful but expensive roofing system. Made from cedar, redwood, or cypress, they are combustible and can rot over a long period of time. Installed cost is about $1.90 per square foot.

CLAY TILE

Clay tile or the newer concrete tile roofing
systems are expensive but provide a
certain strength of character other roofs
seem to lack. They come in a variety of
shapes and colors and require very little
maintenance over the life of the structure.
Clay tile costs about $4.30 per square foot
Concrete costs about $2.75 per square foot

BUILT-UP ROOF

A twenty-year built-up gravel roof is a very inexpensive and dependable roofing system
made up of layers of asphaltic felts bonded
with hot asphalt. A layer of gravel is placed
on the last felt layer to reflect solar heat
and insure proper drainage. This, as well
as a similar coal tar system, is by far
the best for roofs with little or no slope.
Installed cost is about $1.00 per square foot
in place.

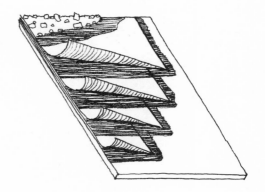

MATERIALS

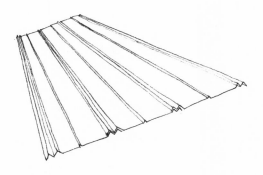

ALUMINUM

Aluminum roofing systems are available that recall the traditional standing seam metal roof at a much reduced price. The price savings are greatest if the roof is simple with few projections and penetrations. Many colors are available. Installed price can be as low as $2.50 per square foot.

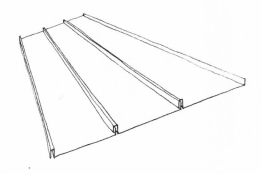

METAL

V-crimp metal roof is another of the less expensive galvanized iron roofing systems which resembles its more expensive brothers. It can be left to its natural patina or can be painted. Installed price is about $2.00 per square foot.

STRUCTURE

Most houses in this country are constructed by carpenters with little use for calculus and maximum moment formulas. A good feel for the material and some common sense will go a long way on the jobsite. This common sense approach is the key to the following chapter on basic structural concepts. However, for unusual loading conditions (such as long spans or cantilevers) or high-tech materials (such as a post-tensioned slab or roof trusses) it is always wise to consult a professional engineer. Structural problems are inexpensive to avoid but very costly to repair after the fact, if repair is possible. Most contractors or fabricators know a good engineer or have one on their staff for this type of consultation.

STRUCTURE

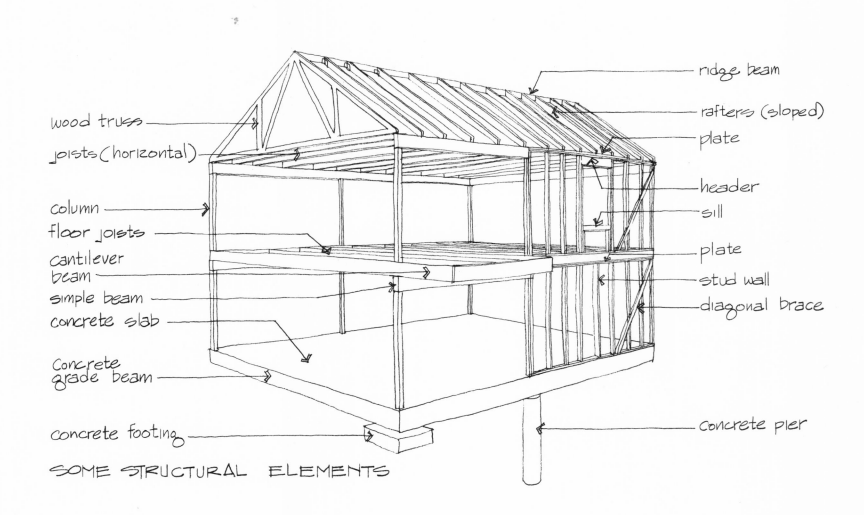

ridge beam

rafters (sloped)

plate

wood truss

joists (horizontal)

header

sill

column

floor joists

plate

cantilever beam

stud wall

simple beam

diagonal brace

concrete slab

Concrete grade beam

concrete footing

concrete pier

SOME STRUCTURAL ELEMENTS

BASEMENT - COLD CLIMATE

Basements are usually found only in northern climes with deep frost lines. The foundation must be below the frost line for stability and a point soon arrives when it is cheaper to utilize the excavated foundation hole than to back-fill it.

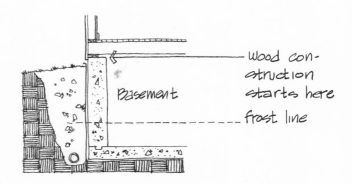

Basement

Wood construction starts here

frost line

PIER AND BEAM - MODERATE CLIMATES

Concrete footings are used to support wood floor systems in more temperate climates. The bottoms must be below the frost line, if any, and on undisturbed soil.

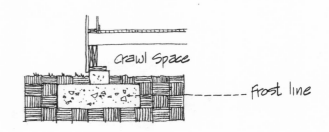

Crawl Space

Frost line

SLAB - ON - GRADE. WARM CLIMATES

Concrete slab on grade is now the accepted norm in warmer climates. Again, the bottom of the outside concrete beam should be below the frost line and resting on undisturbed soil. The foundation subcontractor will design the slab and reinforcing steel if no structural engineer has done a plan.

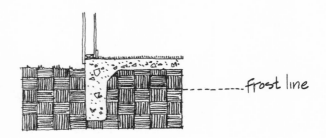

Frost line

STRUCTURE

CONCEPTS

FRAMES

Horizontal frame loading (wind or earthquake) must be resisted by a diagonal brace or membrane capable of transferring these loads to the foundation.

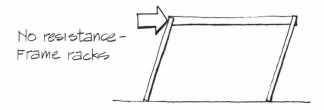

No resistance - Frame racks

These loads can be handled by:

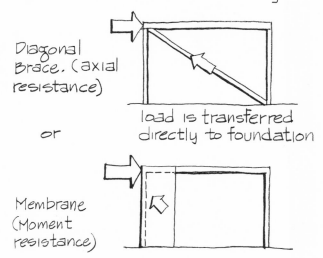

Diagonal Brace. (axial resistance)

or

Membrane (Moment resistance)

load is transferred directly to foundation

COLUMNS

Columns or studs transmit floor and roof loads to the foundation. If the column is too long in comparison to its width it will buckle under the load. This can be corrected by using a fatter column or by bracing.

length to width o.k.

too slender

FOOTINGS

Footings transmit the loads to the ground. Since the earth has a relatively low compressive strength, heavy loads must be distributed over a large area at the foundation or the earth beneath will be compacted. When this compaction takes place, the building settles.

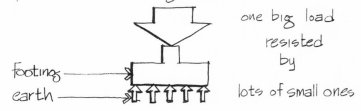

footing

earth

one big load resisted by lots of small ones

120

BEAMS

There are three aspects of beam action to consider when selecting beam, joist or rafter sizes:

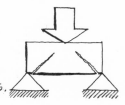

1. <u>shear</u> - the tearing of a beam near the support-usually associated with heavy loads and short spans.

2. <u>Deflection</u>. the sagging of a beam under load - long spans.

3. <u>Moment</u> - splitting of a beam near mid-span - long spans.

Usually, moment or deflection will govern the design of the beam. These failure modes begin in the outermost fibers of the beam cross section, at the top and bottom. The deeper the beam, the less stress on the outer fibers for the same load.

<u>simple span</u>

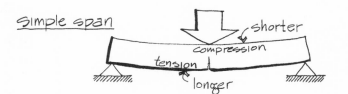

<u>cantilever</u>

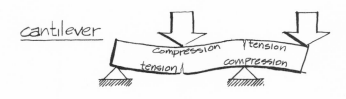

<u>cross-section for simple span</u>

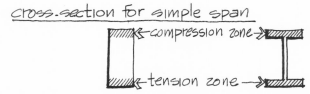

The 'I' section is efficient because it has more fibers or cross-sectional area out at the extremes where they are needed and less in the middle where stresses are low.

STRUCTURE

BEAMS

Almost all houses in the United States are framed with wood stud walls and utilize solid sawn wood beams, girders, and rafters in floors and ceilings. Often a custom plan requires an extra long span which can be accomodated by using a structural engineer and one of the following materials:

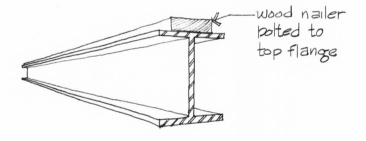

wood nailer
bolted to
top flange

STEEL

A steel beam can span almost any residential space and support whatever loads necessary. It will add expense but that is often a minor cost compared to the spatial flexibility made possible by its use. Steel can be curved or bent for unusual shapes. A steel beam will usually be supported by steel tube columns.

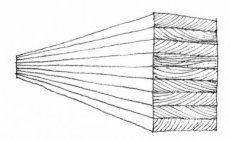

WOOD

A laminated wood beam can accomplish almost the same feats as steel except a slightly larger cross section is required. It will be a little less expensive but may take longer to fabricate.

TRUSSES

Wood roof trusses are the least expensive way to span large distances because they utilize small members which act together as a deep beam. Mechanical and electrical runs can be made between the chords. The truss fabricator will design the proper truss given the span and roof shape. Trusses are also very quick to erect saving on labor costs.

SCISSOR TRUSSES

Scissor trusses allow the economics of truss construction and the aesthetic of the vaulted ceiling.

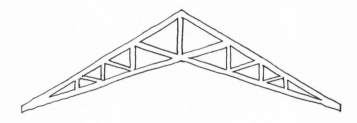

FLAT TRUSSES

Wood floor trusses are similar to the roof truss except the top chord is flat. These can also span a great distance but are often used only because the speed of erection offsets any extra material costs.

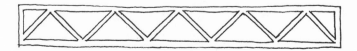

STRUCTURE

JOIST TABLES

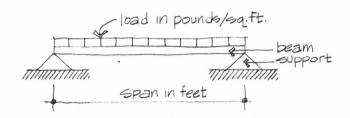

load in pounds/sq.ft.

beam support

span in feet

Maximum spans for solid sawn lumber can be worked out by mathematical formulas. The following chart represents average values for the different lumber sizes and on-center spacings. Calculations of major beams should be delegated to a qualified engineer.

Floor Joists
Live Load = 40 pounds per square foot

Lumber Size	On-center spacing	
	12" o.c.	16" o.c.
2 × 6	11'-0"	9'-6"
2 × 8	14'-6"	12'-6"
2 × 10	18'-0"	16'-0"
2 × 12	21'-6"	19'-0"

Roof Joists or Rafters
Live Load = 20 pounds per square foot

Lumber Size	On-center spacing	
	12" o.c.	16" o.c.
2 × 4	8'-0"	7'-0"
2 × 6	12'-0"	11'-0"
2 × 8	16'-0"	14'-6"
2 × 10	20'-0"	18'-0"
2 × 12	24'-0"	22'-0"

FINANCING

Financing a custom house can be as intricate as designing one in todays world of uncertain interest rates and creative loan packages. In the most common case a home builder will own the lot you want to purchase and he will also build your house. Usually he will already have a long term loan commitment at favorable rates from an institution with which he does business, and financing is no more trouble than filling out the application papers. If one wants to put the job out to competitive bid, financing could be more of a problem. The following pages should give the reader a good idea of the loan amount for which he can qualify and where to obtain it. The contractor can also be depended on to help locate financing so don't fail to use this resource.

FINANCING

How much can I borrow?

Not more than you can repay!

Monthly Payment

The bank has formulas for home loans that are fairly rigid unless you know someone important. To calculate the amount of payment one can be expected to reasonably make, the following ratios are used:

33% of gross annual income for home mortgage
36% of gross annual income for all long term debts (home, car, etc)

Down Payment

The bank also wants protection if the owner defaults on his loan. That protection usually comes as a down payment which offsets the value of the house by 5 to 20%. Usually, they will loan 90% of the appraised value, so, in case of default, the house can be sold at 10% below market value and move quickly.

Calculating actual monthly payments requires a set of amortization tables, area tax and insurance information. A good rule of thumb* that works well for interest rates around 10-12% is that the monthly payment will be approximately 1.0% of the total note on a 30 year loan.

How much can I spend?

Example:

Savings available for the down payment ....$ 20,000.00

Owners gross annual income $40,000.00

Amount available for servicing note:

$40,000 × .33 = $13,200/year

$13,200 ÷ 12 months = $1100/month payment*

Conversion of monthly payment to total amount of note:

$1100. ÷ .01 = $110,000 ....+...$110,000.00

*Rule of thumb ⟶

Total amount owner can spend on house and lot $130,000.00

* Taxes and insurance will increase monthly payment by about $100.00

FINANCING

As interest rates grow, many different types of home loans have become available, some more 'creative' than others. A few of the basic types, in order of interest rates, are listed below:

VA Loan - This loan is made by a local lender but guaranteed by the Veteran's Administration and is available only to veterans although it can be assumed by a non-veteran. This is usually the lowest interest rate available.

FHA Loan - This loan is made by the local lender but guaranteed by the Federal Housing Authority. The bank has a lower risk so interest rates are lower. Houses must meet FHA standards and owners must qualify. Good up to $90,000. This loan can be assumed by the next buyer. Good for resale.

Conventional Loan - This is a typical lending agreement between the lender and the borrower with the house as the only security and no Federal guarantee to back up the loan. Usually ½% more than FHA Loan.

Fixed Rate Loan - Conventional loan with a constant interest rate. Non-assumable.

Variable Rate Loan - This is a conventional loan starting with a low interest rate for the first few years and gradually increasing to a maximum amount. Some are tied to Treasury Bill rates, but be very careful with this type of loan because the deferred interest may be added to the principal, increasing the debt

You will need two loans to build a house. The interim loan will cover the land and construction costs. The completed project must then have a long-term loan (15-30 years). These two types of loans will require two types of lenders.

Banks are more commercial in nature than saving and loans. After a long-term loan commitment has been secured, a bank will be needed for the construction or short-term loan. At the end of the construction period, the bank sells the completed project to the long term lender.

Saving and Loan Institutions may have checking and savings accounts but their main line of business is making long-term, lower interest loans on residential construction. A savings and loan or a mortgage company is where you will find your long-term loan commitment. Find out which ones are familiar with your neighborhood and begin there.

FINANCING

SUB-CONTRACTOR PRICE

Item

1. Material Price.....................Discounted or Contractor Price of Building Materials
   +
2. Labor Price.....................Price of Labor to install material
   +
3. Subcontractor Profit..........Profit margin added by subcontractor 0-20%

total   subcontractor Bid

GENERAL CONTRACTOR PRICE

4. Subcontractor Bid............From above
   +
5. Other subs Bids..............Similar to above
   +
6. General Contractor Profit.....Margin required by General to supervise work (5-20%)
   +
7. General Contractor Overhead...Job shack, telephone, Port-a-can, electrical, insurance, bonds, etc.

Total   Total Price to Owner

Items 3, 6, and 7 are usually a percentage function of the preceding totals. All profit amounts are negotiable to the extent that the contractor needs the job.

Banks and savings and loans do not stay in business by making bad loans. They build in all the protection they can. Other details which can be problems are:

House Type

The lender will review your house plans and expects to see a 3 bedroom-2 bath house that he can resale easily in case of default. This makes it more difficult to finance anything too custom unless it can be converted easily. It helps if the owner will increase his equity (larger down payment) or knows the banker's brother.

Raw Land Loan

A loan on raw land (the lot) is difficult for an individual to obtain because the vacant property may be hard to unload if the owner defaults. The bank may make the loan to your contractor along with the construction loan. This way they have made the total loan on a finished project that can be sold more easily. Usually, they will not make this loan until the long-term financing has been arranged.

FINANCING

Most contractors are honest businessmen but they dislike (1) to lose a job, and (2) to work for nothing. The following items can become real problems unless the owner has considered them beforehand.

Remodel and Renovation Costs are very difficult to estimate since many conditions are unknown and are almost always the worst case. Any contractor will work at cost plus an hourly rate but if a maximum ceiling price is required, it will always be inflated with contingencies to cover unknown areas.

Allowances are used for equipment prices if the owner has not had time to select the actual brand. If the selected type is cheaper, money goes back to owner.

Change Orders. Many changes occur during construction as the owner sees the house take shape and wants to add a detail here or move a window there. Some are no trouble to the contractor and can be done at no charge. However, many contractors bid very low to get the job and depend upon costly change orders to make up his profit. This is always a major area of concern for an owner without professional guidance and can be quite expensive.

CONTRACTOR

Never underestimate the difficulty of orchestrating a complex job involving many people and getting each one to perform at the right time, not to mention solving technical problems in a slab while the concrete is hardening. The contractors job is not an easy one but it is one that more and more homeowners are electing to take on themselves. The following chapter gives a brief job description for the contractor and some hints about the job. See suggested reference books for help in this area.

CONTRACTOR

Do-it-yourself-contracting can be a good idea
for the following reasons:

♫ I did it my way! ♪

(1) A good deal, if not all of the work can be done by an owner with common
sense, a good how-to book, and a lot of patience and time.
(2) A great deal of money can be saved both in labor hours and profit.
(3) A feeling of satisfaction can be derived from learning, doing, and physical labor.
(4) Quality control can be maintained with an owner on the job.

Do-it-yourself-contracting does have a down side:

Where are those guys?

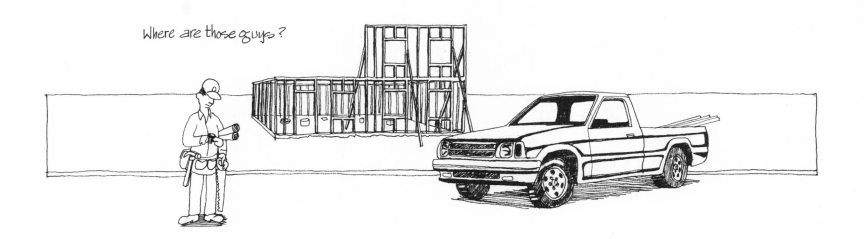

(1) It's your house, you may be too emotionally attached to it for objectivity.

(2) You may not have the right experience or a list of responsible subcontractors.

(3) Refer to subcontractor description, this section.

(4) Refer to general contractor description, this section.

CONTRACTOR

GENERAL CONTRACTOR

Where are those guys?

The general contractor is an independant businessman, but usually more responsible than many subcontractors. His job is to select subcontractors he can depend upon, gather their bids, and schedule the construction sequence. He is responsible for getting the subs on and off the job at the right time and making sure the work is done in the correct manner. He makes draws from the bank and pays subcontractors and material suppliers. He usually can be found with a bottle of aspirin in his pocket.

SUBCONTRACTOR

Where is that guy?

The subcontractor is usually an independant businessman with a pick-up and a small crew specializing in one of the building trades. His responsibility is to arrive on the job at his scheduled time with the correct materials, do his job well, and make way for the next sub's task. He is usually unorganized, with jobs spread all over the city and many people clamoring for his attention. He can usually be found on someone else's job.

CONTRACTOR

CONTRACTOR / OWNER LEVERS

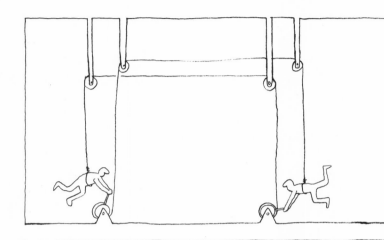

The relationship between the contractor and the owner should be one of reasonable understanding on both sides. If one party takes unfair advantage, the whole project will suffer, and both parties lose. Some levers to control the relationship are built-into the contract as follows:

Payments called 'draws' are made periodically by the lender to the General Contractor. The lender will usually have a representative make an on-site inspection before a draw is granted to verify that the work has been done and materials are in place. The General should be allowed to draw 90% of his total due at any one time. The held 10% ensures his continuing interest in completing the work on time and correctly.

Warranties come with building systems such as roofs, mechanical equipment and household appliances. They are only as good as their warrantor.

Mechanics Liens can be legally attached to a property by any unpaid sub-contractor. This can prevent the sale of the property until the suit is settled. Make sure your General Contractor pays his Subs

PRACTICAL DESIGN

The following pages contain ideas of a
practical nature which should be considered
in every house design. Among these items
are typical heights, widths, sizes, and shapes,
as well as principles of sun, wind, and codes.
One does not need to observe these practical
rules as much as one should be aware of
them, however they usually represent concepts
that are time-tested. They will save you
money as well as make life more comfortable.

PRACTICAL DESIGN

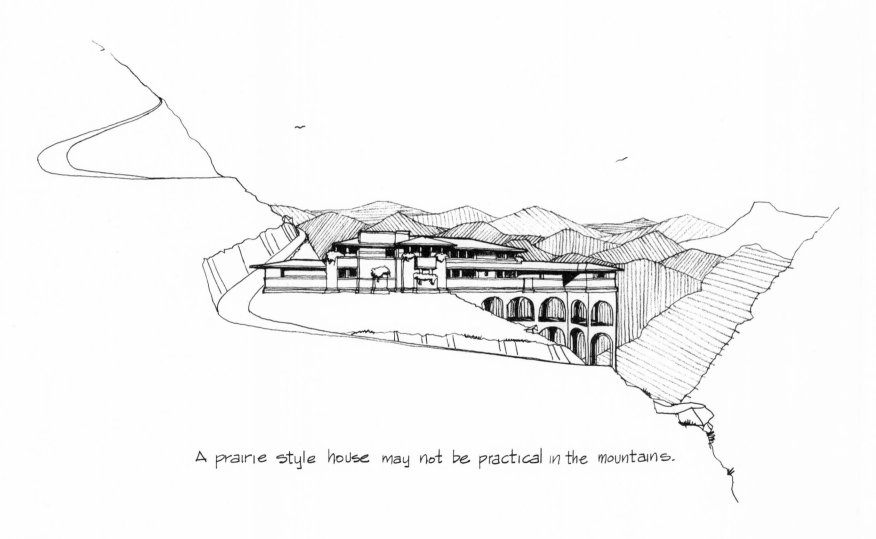

A prairie style house may not be practical in the mountains.

There are several versions of basic building codes and each local authority usually makes minor addendums to the one they select. These codes are generally concerned with commercial buildings and all say about the same thing. The main area of regulation for residential construction is exiting requirements for fire, some of which are described below:

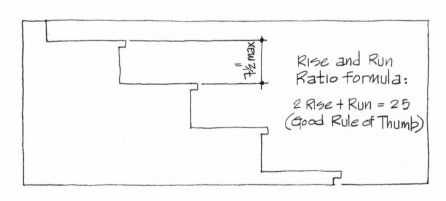

7½" max

Rise and Run Ratio formula:

2 Rise + Run = 25
(Good Rule of Thumb)

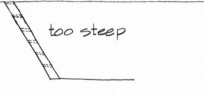

too steep

tread width varies too much.

Ships Ladder or spiral stair cannot be counted as exits from sleeping areas - They are O.K. for studies, playrooms, etc.

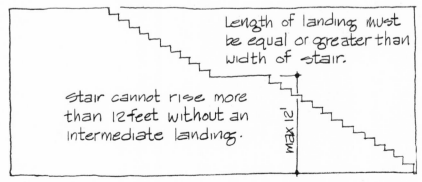

Length of landing must be equal or greater than width of stair.

Stair cannot rise more than 12 feet without an intermediate landing.

max 12'

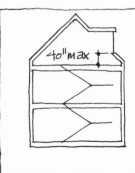

40" max

Third floor sleeping areas must have 2 exits - One standard stair and one window or skylight opening onto roof will usually meet code requirements.

PRACTICAL DESIGN

WIND

In many climates a properly designed house can use natural ventilation for cooling during a large part of the year. Moving air around a body increases the evaporation rate, absorbing heat and lowering the body temperature. It also removes air heated by the heat sources within the house. Therefore, it is important to understand how to keep air moving.

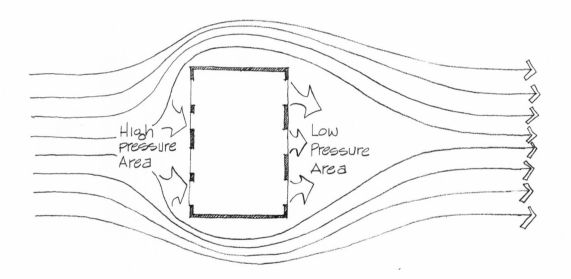

A house is ventilated not by wind forcing its way through windows and cracks, but by the flow of air around the structure creating a low pressure area on the leeward side of the house. This low pressure area pulls air out of the house creating an interior low pressure area which in turn pulls air into the house from the higher pressure area. Therefore natural ventilation design tells us to broadside the prevailing winds during the clement periods and place large openings on the broad sides.

A closed attic space can collect a lot of heat, which is helpful in winter months. In summer months, however, operable louvers can be opened to ventilate the attic separately from the house, providing a cool **zone** between living areas and the sun.

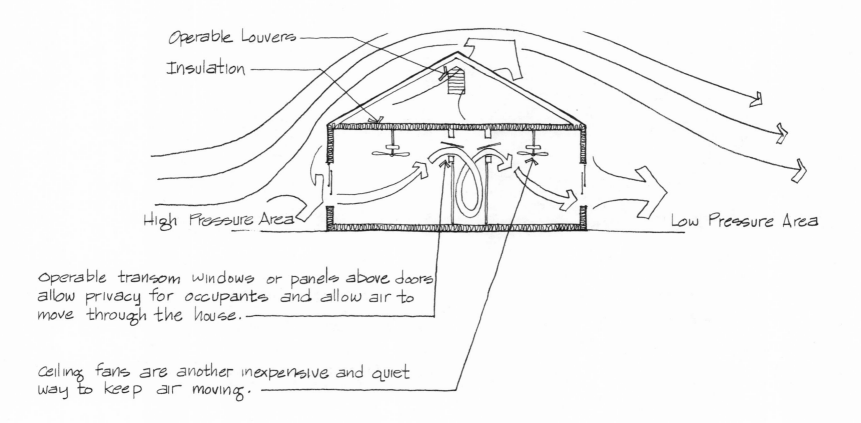

Operable Louvers

Insulation

High Pressure Area

Low Pressure Area

Operable transom windows or panels above doors allow privacy for occupants and allow air to move through the house.

Ceiling fans are another inexpensive and quiet way to keep air moving.

PRACTICAL DESIGN

SOLAR CHARTS

The solar path for any latitude can be determined from solar charts found in Architectural Graphic standards or any solar book. This chart shows the solar angle and altitude at any hour of the year. This information can help a designer accurately develop solar shading devices for the building.

40° Latitude

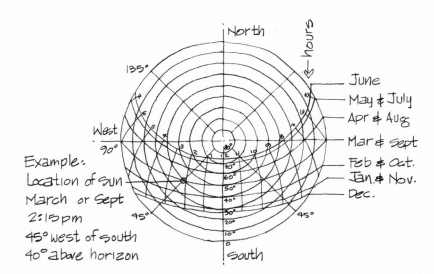

Example:
Location of sun
March or Sept
2:15pm
45° west of south
40° above horizon

Solar Chart for 40° Latitude

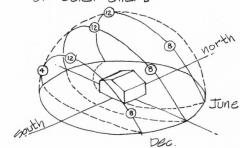

Three Dimensional Projection of Solar Chart

The basic information necessary for a designer can be distilled to two points:

1. In winter, the sun is low in the south and sets south of west.

2. In summer, the sun is high in the sky and sets north of west.

PRACTICAL DESIGN

Study of solar radiation values will verify that the optimum orientation for any building will be long axis east-west or broad sides facing north and south. In winter, this allows maximum surface area maximum solar exposure (south wall), and in summer, minimum surface area at locations of maximum solar exposure (east and west walls).

Even without actively designing for solar energy, there are some basics that will help a designer plan for optimum orientation. The diagrams show relative amounts of heat gain on each surface of a building for 40° latitude (ave. U.S.)

In areas with hot days and cold nights, a slightly south-eastern tilt may be beneficial. This will allow more exposure in the mornings to assist a rapid heat-up and a glancing shot from the western sun in the evenings.

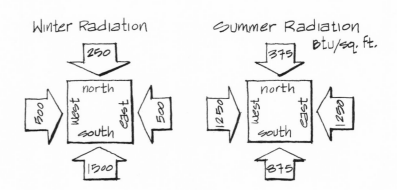

Winter Radiation   Summer Radiation

Btu/sq. ft.

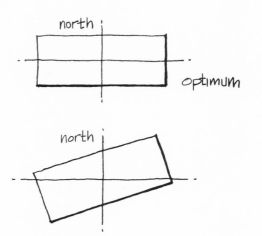

PRACTICAL DESIGN

SOLAR SHADING

Direct solar radiation can be very warming and cheerful or it can create a large air conditioning problem, depending on the time of the year. It can be effectively controlled by mechanical means such as blinds or drapes, but there are also more natural and effective ways. It is always better to intercept solar radiation before it enters the house.

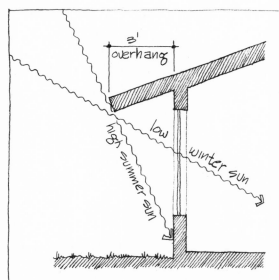

The sun is high in the summer and low in the southern sky in the winter. This seasonal variation in solar angle can be used to great advantage in residential design.

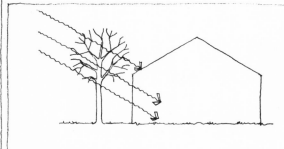

Deciduous trees (oaks, maples, pecans, etc) lose their leaves in the fall allowing the winter solar radiation to penetrate the house.

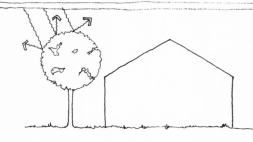

During hot summer months the foliage absorbs and reflects incoming solar radiation.

PRACTICAL DESIGN

Since most houses have a sloped roof, a designer
should consider the desirability of utilizing that
attic space for a future expansion. This option
can be kept open at very little extra initial
cost by providing enough slope for headroom,
routing air ducts around the perimeter of the
attic, and using beams, joists, and rafters
instead of the more standard roof trusses.

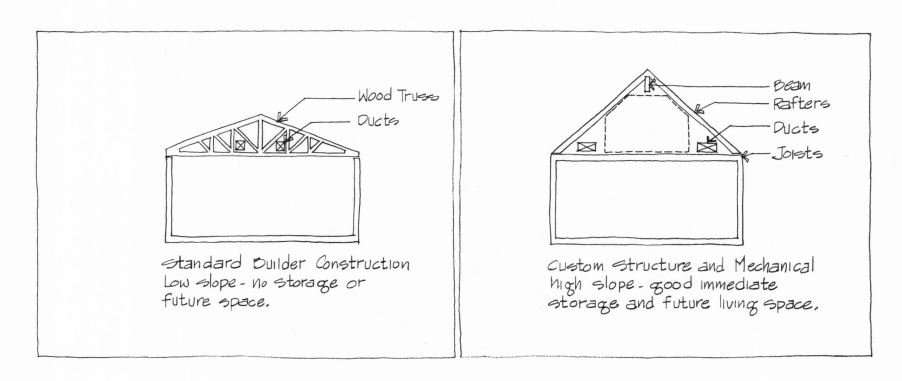

Wood Truss

Ducts

Beam

Rafters

Ducts

Joists

Standard Builder Construction
Low slope - no storage or
future space.

Custom Structure and Mechanical
high slope - good immediate
storage and future living space.

PRACTICAL DESIGN

DOORS

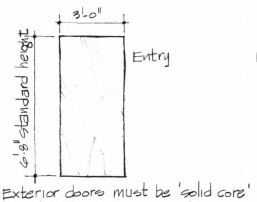

Entry

Exterior doors must be 'solid core' (noted s.c.) which means they are a solid wood slab, strong, heavy, and cost a little extra.

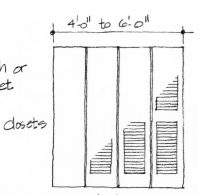

Bedroom

Bath or Closet

closets

Interior doors can be solid core or hollow core (h.c.) which means they are a wood veneer on a honeycomb structure.

Bi-fold doors are best for closet applications and other large interior openings. Can be hollow core or louvered.

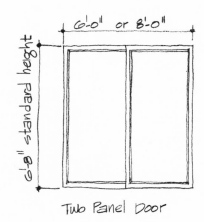

Two Panel Door

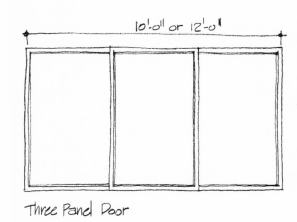

Three Panel Door

Aluminum Sliding Glass Doors are a very economical way to enclose space. They are weather-proof, provide a great amount of light, view, and an entry, low-maintenance, and come with tempered glass for safety.

PRACTICAL DESIGN

Window type and material must be selected to complement the house design, the owner's lifestyle, and the budget. Consideration must be given to security, ventilation, cleaning, style, etc. Most architects prefer the awning window because it opens 100% and shields itself from rain when open. Residential frames are manufactured in wood, aluminum, steel, and even plastic and most types are available in double and/or triple glazing. (see appendix)

Single or Double Hung   Horizontal Slider

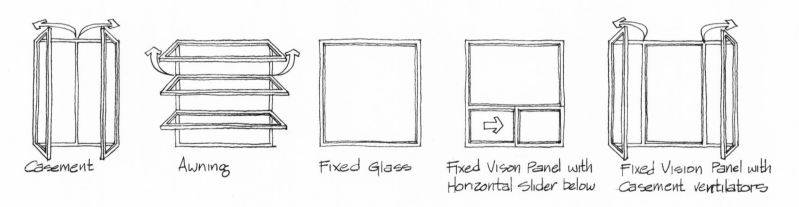

Casement   Awning   Fixed Glass   Fixed Vison Panel with   Fixed Vision Panel with
                                                  Horizontal Slider below   Casement ventilators

Windows come in almost any width and height combination from 2' to 6'. Fixed glass will be cut to size and may be cut round, arched, or angled.

PRACTICAL DESIGN

PLUMBING WALLS

Plumbing must have cold and/or hot water supply, be vented and drained. A typical vent will require a 6" stud wall for proper installation and roof flashing. A designer can save money by arranging plumbing walls in a back-to-back fashion to share supply, vent, and drain lines.

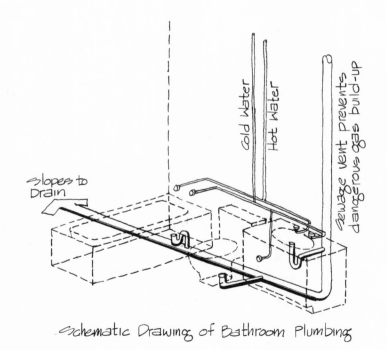

Schematic Drawing of Bathroom Plumbing

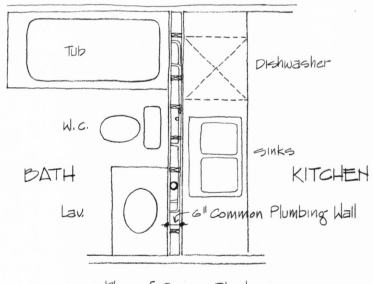

Plan of Common Plumbing

Cabinets come stock in standard sizes and styles or can be custom designed and fabricated which can become expensive. The drawings show standard dimensions which can be modified slightly at little cost.

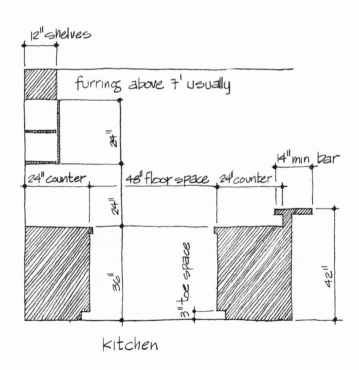

Kitchen

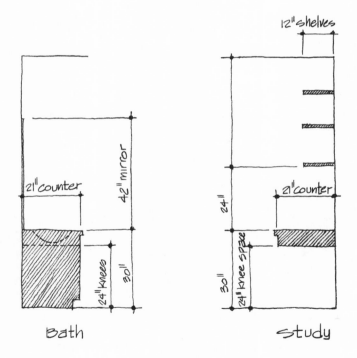

Bath   Study

PRACTICAL DESIGN

CEILING HEIGHT

8'-0" has become accepted as the standard residential ceiling height in the U.S. mainly because that is the modular length of gypsum board or plywood. It is a comfortable height for the smaller spaces found in most houses. A higher ceiling is necessary in a larger space and can make smaller spaces seem larger.

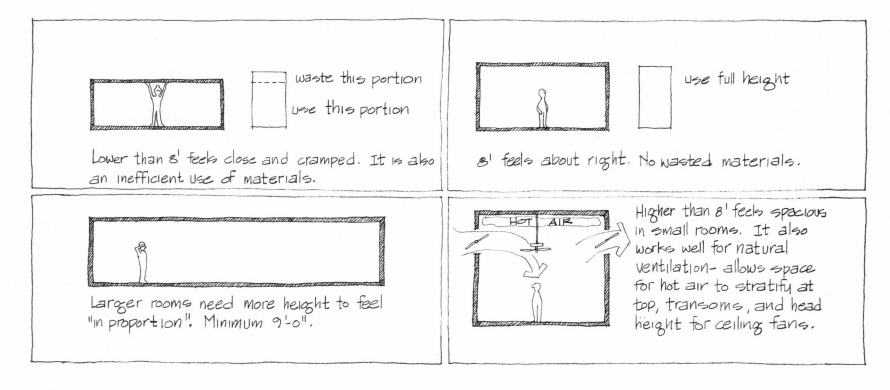

waste this portion
use this portion

Lower than 8' feels close and cramped. It is also an inefficient use of materials.

use full height

8' feels about right. No wasted materials.

Larger rooms need more height to feel "in proportion". Minimum 9'-0".

HOT   AIR

Higher than 8' feels spacious in small rooms. It also works well for natural ventilation- allows space for hot air to stratify at top, transoms, and head height for ceiling fans.

AESTHETIC DESIGN

The preceding chapters contain most of the information necessary to design a house to meet your practical needs and ideas. This is where most people who design for themselves happily stop. For the reader who would like to do more, this is the beginning. It is the point where architecture diverges from mere building. We must become more aware of space if we are to experience it and in turn design that experience. An architect can spend his life refining spatial concepts and relationships. It is a learning process rooted in symbols and cultural meaning on the more abstract levels and a constant awareness on the physical level. The following pages give a brief overview of the basic principles of spatial theory to make the designer more conscious of the powerful tools at his disposal and give examples of how they have been used by some experts.

AESTHETIC DESIGN

SHAPE · PLAN

The object of architecture is not so much to erect a structure, but to create the space within and around that structure. All space will have some amount of emotional content associated with it and it is the architect's job to produce the correct emotional content by manipulating the various elements that define space. One of the major definers of space is form, which may give the observer direct instructions.

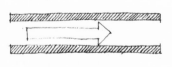 A slender form suggests movement.

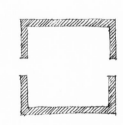 Equal sides have a restful quality but may become static and boring.

 Circular or octagonal forms tend to make an observer want to stop and find the center. May suggest introspection or self-conciousness.

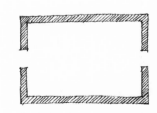 A form slightly longer than wide tends to be restful and interesting.

Ceiling form may suggest emotional content in the following ways:

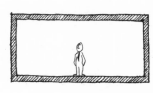

A flat ceiling is relatively neutral unless it is too low or sags in the middle.

A pitched ceiling forces our eyes and emotions upward. Feels light and spacious.

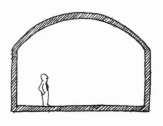

An arched ceiling or vault has an inherent structural strength. Feels secure and embracing. Always interesting.

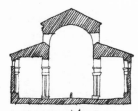

S. Giorgio Maggiore

The expert combination of form, volume, and shape is a basic ingredient in the architecture of the worlds great spaces.

AESTHETIC DESIGN

SHAPE and VOLUME

The third dimension of form is another major determinant of the emotional content. This aspect of space can be subdivided into components of volume and shape. The volume of a space is related to scale and may also have strong emotional significance.

A low ceiling, like an overcast day, can be oppressive and depressing.

A low ceiling in combination with a small room can have serious repercussions.

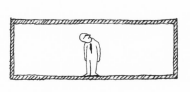

A higher than average ceiling can feel uplifting and energetic. It can also make small rooms feel larger and more spacious.

A very high ceiling can overpower an observer, inducing a feeling of awe and humility.

AESTHETIC DESIGN

The emotional content of space is dependent upon the human experience and it is for this reason that scale is a major determinant of architecture.
scale is the implicit size of a thing relative to its measurer - the human observer.

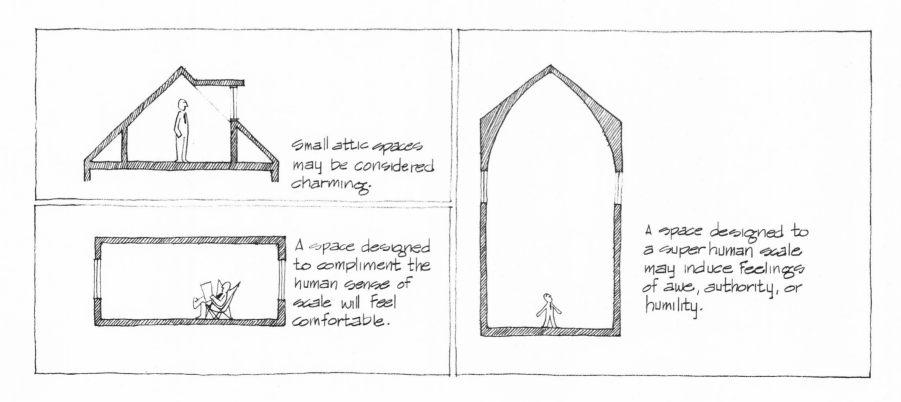

Small attic spaces may be considered charming.

A space designed to compliment the human sense of scale will feel comfortable.

A space designed to a super human scale may induce feelings of awe, authority, or humility.

AESTHETIC DESIGN

SCALE

Scale may also be taken relative to an intermediary object which is of a known size to the human observer, like a door or another building.

Il Redentore - Venice
Andrea Palladio

From a distance, the size of the building will be difficult to guess since it is in proportion with the door and portico, but to a superhuman scale.

The large house is out of scale with its human occupant and out of proportion with its neighborhood.

If scale is the measure of things relative to the human observer, then proportion may be thought of as the measure of things relative to each other and to the whole. Many systems have been devised to help determine 'correct and harmonious proportion. A few of these are noted below:

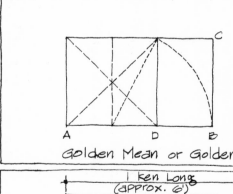

Golden Mean or Golden Section

This proportion was discovered by the classical Greeks and is often found in nature.

$$\frac{AB}{BC} = \frac{AB + BC}{AB} = 1.618$$

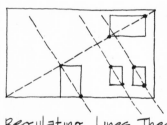

Regulating Lines Theory

This system employs diagonal lines or their perpendiculars to produce rectangles of equal proportions.

I Ken Long
(approx. 6')

½ Ken Wide
(approx 3')

The Ken or Tatami

The Japanese Ken is a 1:2 proportioned module used to describe the size and shape of rooms in human scale.

The Modulor

The Modulor is a system of proportion created by Le Corbusier consisting of measurements taken from the circle and square and related to man.

AESTHETIC DESIGN

PROPORTION

While the rules of scale may be successfully violated to achieve certain desired results, the violation of the laws of proportion is usually uncomfortable and displeasing to the human eye.

Window too large in proportion to size of house and door.

Column too short and fat.

Too tall and thin.

Many of the proportioning systems are based on the human body.

Column about right relative to human proportions. Column of Trajan

The comparative roughness or smoothness of materials has strong psychological implications for the spaces they define. We do not need to touch a rough stone to know that it can snag our clothes. This message is a subtle limitation to the 'personal space' within which we feel comfortable, and this can make a room seem smaller and more confining.

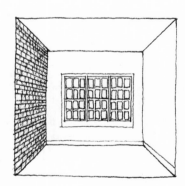

One textured wall can add variety and interest to a room - a feeling of solidity.

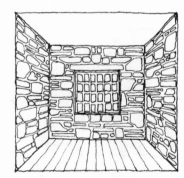

Four walls with heavy texture can become uncomfortably small.

AESTHETIC DESIGN

NATURAL LIGHT

The experience of space is a direct result of the information received through the senses and passed on to the brain. A large portion of this sensory input is visual stimulation which means that light, as a communication medium, has a very powerful role in the technical as well as the emotional experience of architecture. Textures and shapes are read through light and shadow. Any space can be vastly altered by the size, shape, and placement of openings.

Small openings may make a room seem cozy or confining.

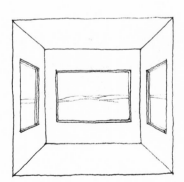

Large openings give an exciting and spacious feeling.

Natural light can be skillfully manipulated in many ways to achieve many different and dramatic effects. The combination of large interior volume and dim lighting (controlled by size of opening and trans-lucence of glass) is used to produce some of the world's greatest and most moving architectural spaces. This concept is often used to symbolize both the greatness and mystery of God in architecture.

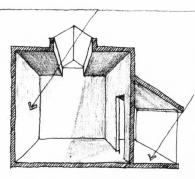

skylight allows direct light into interior rooms.

Floor to ceiling opening on south side creates a welcome warm sunny space in winter.

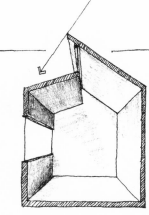

Indirect clerestory light is especially good for artist studios

High opening on north wall is almost as good but light plume cannot reach far.

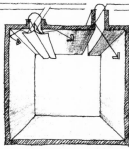

skylights can be controlled to admit only indirect light by using baffles or light shafts.

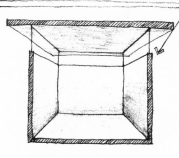

Clerestory around edge of roof provides maximum light and privacy. Allows roof plane to 'float' above wall.

AESTHETIC DESIGN

COLOR

Once we have determined the size, shape, and placement of wall openings, we have determined the amount of light allowed into the space. Now we must decide if that light is absorbed or reflected—which can offset or amplify the lighting condition at the wall. This is done with color.

Colors also have psychological implications. Bright warm colors, especially reds, are associated with energy while cool colors, such as blue or green, have restful connotations. However, a wise decision for amature colorists would be to use a subtle white or light gray basic color, make the ceiling a shade lighter than the walls, and employ a stronger color for trim, detail, or accent.

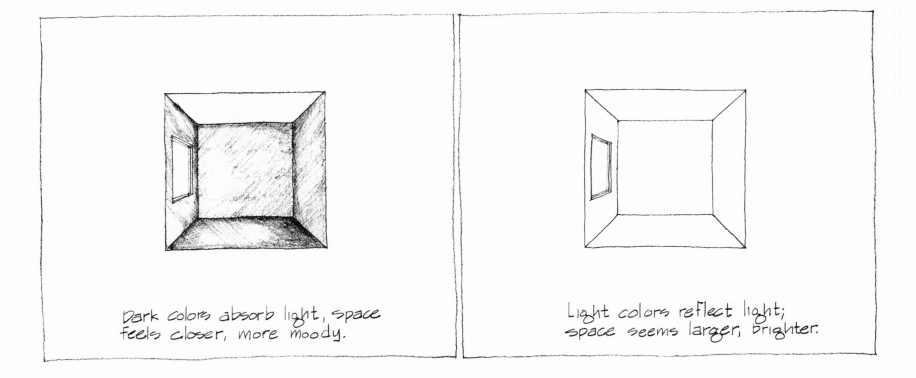

Dark colors absorb light, space feels closer, more moody.

Light colors reflect light; space seems larger, brighter.

Color can be used successfully as a more active design tool to articulate a wall or an architectural element. It can also become a design element for ornamentation to make a large bare wall more interesting. Any use of color should be exercised with great care. When in doubt, stick to light shades of gray or earth tones.

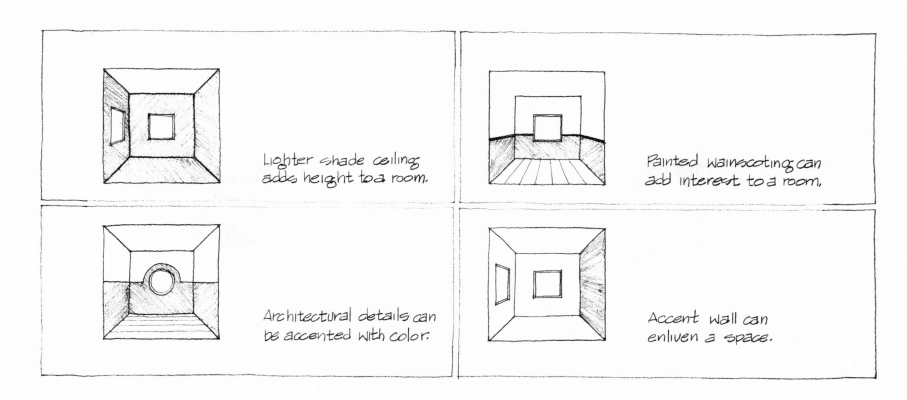

Lighter shade ceiling adds height to a room.

Painted wainscoting can add interest to a room.

Architectural details can be accented with color.

Accent wall can enliven a space.

AESTHETIC DESIGN

ACOUSTICS

Just as color will absorb or reflect light, changing the mood in a space, so do different materials absorb or reflect sound, thereby affecting the comfort level. Each space should be acoustically balanced its function by varying the amount and location of soft absorptive materials or hard, reflective materials.

Families with children may be more comfortable with wall to wall carpet, overstuffed furniture, and drapes.

Music rooms are brighter and truer with hard-wood floors and reflective surfaces.

AESTHETIC DESIGN

The perception of order seems to be an intuitively basic human desire. There are some elementary principles which help a designer create a sense of order and in turn, they provide direction to the designer. They are simple methods of organization which have evolved along with western culture and although all are still valid, most can be idenified with a particular period in history.

The following pages describe the ordering concepts which can give form and provide meaning to an otherwise arbitrary arrangement of diverse spaces. Of course, like a picket fence, too rigid an order may become boring. The rules may be broken with exciting results but one has more success in this endeavor if one breaks a rule with a specific purpose rather than by accident or through ignorance.

AESTHETIC DESIGN

AXIAL

This is an ordering concept very similar to the idea of 'lining things up'. It implies the existance of an axis or line with elements distributed along that line. In planning, the line is a path of movement such as a road or corridor. The procession along that line determines the experience and the view down the corridor usually requires a strong architectural element to suitably terminate the movement.

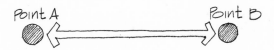

This is the simplest relationship between two elements and its potential strength is magnificiently apparent in the city of Paris. The axis are set up in series between monuments and the total plan in this case becomes a constellation arrangement with interconnecting axis.

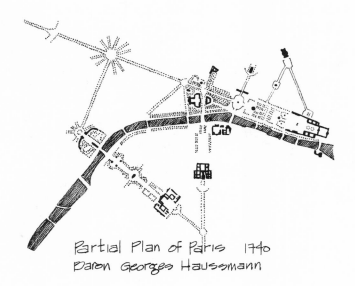

Partial Plan of Paris 1740
Baron Georges Haussmann

The residential equivalent of the axial organization can take one of two forms. Both use the axis as an organizational line for the ordering of space.

In the first case the axis is used in the same manner as in the plan of Paris. It is a link between two points which in turn serve as anchor to the axis.

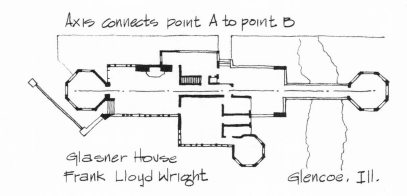

Axis connects point A to point B

Glasner House
Frank Lloyd Wright   Glencoe, Ill.

In the second, perhaps more functional and modern use, the axis becomes a physical link or corridor. It is now a path of movement along which the spaces are distributed. This organization easily solves the zoning and privacy problems. The axis termination can be accomodated with a window, a sculpture niche, or even a special door treatment. This axis is called a "spine."

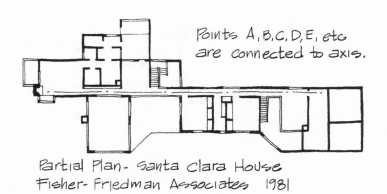

Points A,B,C,D,E, etc are connected to axis.

Partial Plan- Santa Clara House
Fisher- Friedman Associates   1981

AESTHETIC DESIGN

CLUSTER

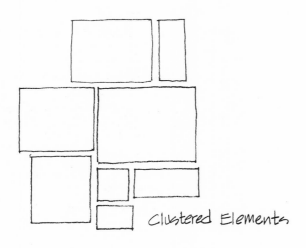

Clustered Elements

This is a very old organizational principle in which elements are clustered or grouped around a central circulation core, or in some cases just each other. This principle is highly visible in many old villages with their meandering alleyways and tightly grouped buildings.

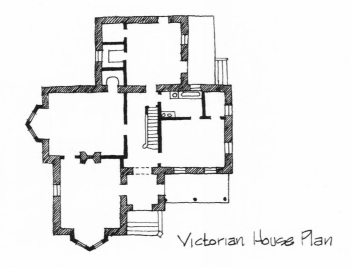

Victorian House Plan

Clustered elements were the prevailing concept in American housing until Frank Lloyd Wright resurrected the axial plan with the Usonian Houses and corridor organization.

AESTHETIC DESIGN

The central plan is a refinement of the cluster organization in which smaller secondary elements are grouped around a larger central element. This produces a hierarchy of spaces that can be helpful in the exterior massing composition. It has long been a prominent organizational concept in Eastern church architecture and was employed in the grand residential achievements by Palladio and his many followers.

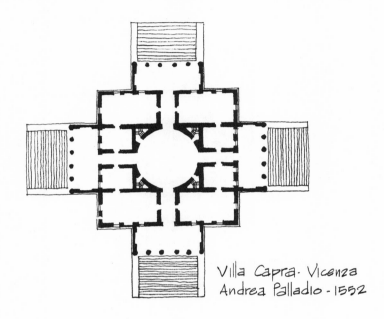

Villa Capra. Vicenza
Andrea Palladio - 1552

A modern version of the Villa Capra (Rotonda) might reflect the propensity for Americans to congregate in the kitchen, replacing the living room as the social center of life at home.

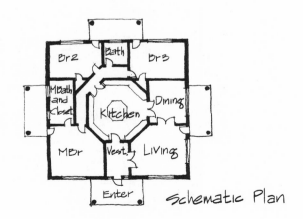

Schematic Plan

AESTHETIC DESIGN

GRID

This concept so predominant in American city planing was introduced by the Romans in their military camps. It's repetitive nature gives it a natural cohesion and several grid units can be combined to produce a hierarchy of spaces and experiences.

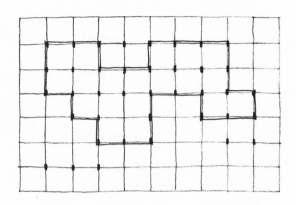

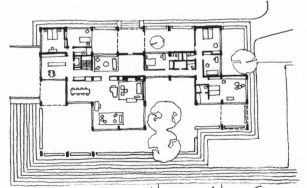

Eric Boissonnas House - New Canaan
Philip Johnson - 1956

The module can be selected for its structural efficiency and can greatly reduce structural costs; however, the designer is locked in once he begins and loses spatial flexibility for the different functions, since space must be added or subtracted in modular units.

This concept may involve a combination of the central and axial principles employing the central element for hierarchy with smaller elements distributed along axis connected to the central element. Another variation is the pinwheel concept of similar spaces radiating about a central point. The actual plan will likely be some combination of all three.

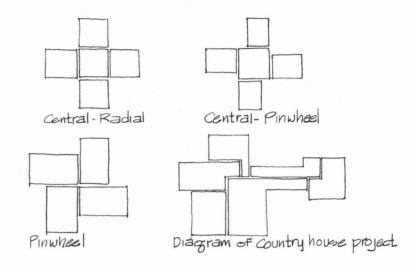

Central-Radial Central-Pinwheel

Pinwheel Diagram of Country house project

The modular aspect of the pinwheel radial plan make it very attractive for planning with manufactured housing units or for four-plex designs.

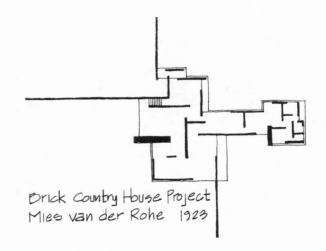

Brick Country House Project
Mies van der Rohe 1923

AESTHETIC DESIGN

SUPERIMPOSED GRID

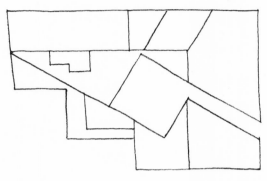

Plan Diagram

A grid system produces a set of orthogonal reference points which, conciously or unconciously, provide a sense of order to the observer. This rather rigid form of organization can become too predictable and boring. Overlaying one grid over another produces two sets of orthogonal reference points which can be played one against the other to stimulate interest in the observer.

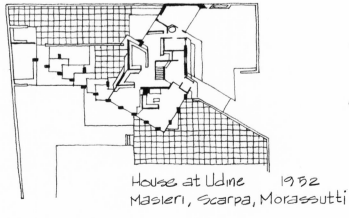

House at Udine   1952
Masieri, Scarpa, Morassutti

This type of ordering system is a relatively recent concept, probably dating back to the city plan for Washington, D.C. by L'Enfant in which a system of radial diagonals are superimposed over a rectangular grid creating a magnificient city fabric with strong axial links and strange street intersections.

AESTHETIC DESIGN

Like any other artistic endevor, architecture concerns itself with a balanced composition. The balancing of the building masses allows the eye to see the individual forms as part of a whole, complete and not wanting for additions. This can be done by allowing a room or a group of rooms to be read in elevation as single elements distinct from the other rooms. These massing elements can be thought of as weights on a slab supported on a pivot located near the center.

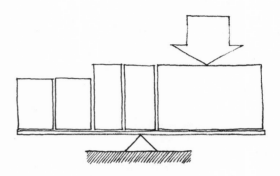

Unbalanced composition is unstable, wants to tilt to the right, creating a tension within the observer.

Varying the masses of elements creates a heirarchy among them. Usually the largest or most important interior space is expressed as the largest mass. This dominant mass, when properly balanced within the whole, can create a unity from the parts. This is successful composition.

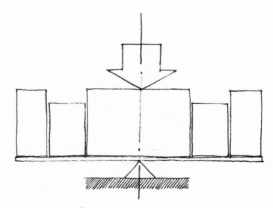

Balanced composition is stable and in restful equilibrium.

AESTHETIC DESIGN

SYMMETRICAL COMPOSITION

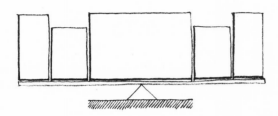

classical symmetry - Perfect balance

In a symmetrical composition, smaller elements are distributed in a similar fashion to each side of the center, creating a mirror image about the center of the composition. This is usually employed with a larger element at the center, creating a strong sense of heirarchy and dominance, and therefore unity.

Pisani castle by Palladio

A symmetrical or near symmetrical composition is by far the easiest form of massing in architecture. It was prevalent throughout the classical periods, and is still highly regarded today, especially in the more monumental buildings.

AESTHETIC DESIGN

Hierarchy and dominance are still key words in an asymmetrical arrangement of elements but this form of massing is balanced by adjustments in the proportions and apparent weight of the various elements and their relationships to each other.

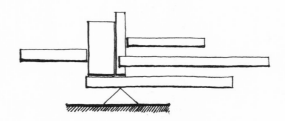

Asymmetrical Composition - Dynamic Balance

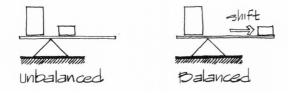

Unbalanced   Balanced

Smaller elements can be shifted outward from the fulcrum until they seem to balance larger elements opposite the support. Overlapping and penetration can be useful balancing techniques in this most difficult of composition methods.

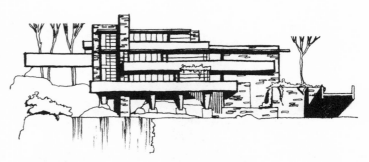

South Elevation - Kaufman House
Frank Lloyd Wright   1936

177

AESTHETIC DESIGN

MASSING

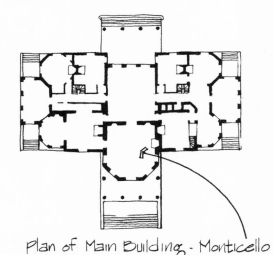

Plan of Main Building - Monticello

Monticello - Virginia
Thomas Jefferson - 1770

The object of massing is to produce an interesting building shape which creates a pleasing and balanced composition from every view and also reveals something of the spaces inside. Although it would be possible to lump several small elements together to create a single major exterior mass, it would not be considered honest. An architectural statement is considered honest when large interior spaces read as major elements in the massing of the building and vice versa. In this way the exterior of the building is an honest expression of the interior spaces.

The major space in the plan reads as the major element in the massing. We have some idea about the plan by studying the exterior.

The two basic approaches to massing are called additive and subtractive. The end result is usually some combination of the two.

SUBTRACTIVE MASSING

In this method, the building is thought of as a single, whole element (usually a geometric solid) which may be subdivided or subtracted from to reveal its inner self. In the search for order, the eye will fill in the missing parts and see the whole solid as the unity of the composition.

This method was a basic tenet in the International school of modern architecture which was founded in part by Le Corbusier. He believed that the Platonic solids were basic to man's inner self and the most beautiful of all forms.

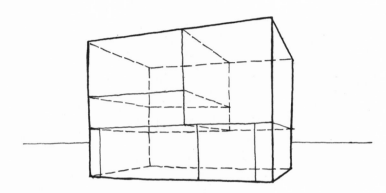

Maison shodhan · Ahmedabad
Le Corbusier - 1956

AESTHETIC DESIGN

ADDITIVE MASSING

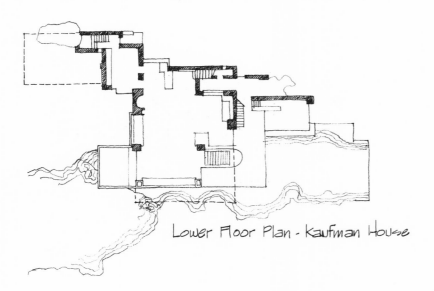

Lower Floor Plan - Kaufman House

This form of massing can be defined as the addition of small pieces until their sum creates a unified whole. This is similar to the plan method of considering each space as a separate element and placing them together to create functional as well as massing relationships.

Kaufmann House (Falling Water) - Bear Run, Pennsylvania
Frank Lloyd Wright - 1936

This method can be used to stack and compose individual masses into a complete whole as shown in the Kaufman House. It was used in another sense by Renaissance masters to build-up facades with various geometric shapes within strict mathematical and proportional systems.

The regular spacing of events along a line is a basic form of order found in our conception of time, the cycles of the moon, and also in the principles of architecture. The regular repetition of an element allows an observer to expect the next element and thereby understand an order to the system. This repetition occurs most commonly in the spacing of columns and in the placement of openings.

A strong rhythm amplifies the formality of a building.

Parthenon - Athens

This repetition can also happen in the recurrence of a certain proportion throughout the composition by use of the regulating line theories or other proportioning systems.

A more complex rhythm can be more interesting for the eye.

Basilica - Vicenza

AESTHETIC DESIGN

LINING THINGS UP

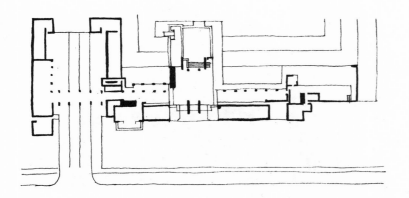

A major portion of the human condition concerns itself with the search for order within the apparent chaos. Order can be understood and this understanding of our environment makes us feel secure. The eye wants to find order by creating relationships between elements. One of the most basic of these relationships is the alignment of closely related objects or 'lining things up'.

House on the Mesa
Frank Lloyd Wright 1932

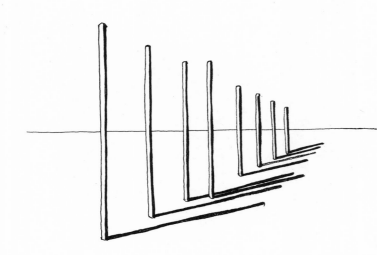

It can be disturbing when something seems like it should line and doesn't.

STYLE

After we have solved the functional and aesthetic problems of the plan and building mass, we may want to render our design in a particular style which expresses our individuality to ourselves and to others. Almost all styles are representative of a certain historical time and culture. They may be born for one set of reasons and revived at a later period for another, but they are always an embellishment of the basic structure and make a statement about the inhabitant.

The Modern Style may be thought of as a stylistic rebellion against style. On the other hand, one may borrow liberally from many styles as in the Post Modern Movement or simply attempt to eliminate any particular style in favor of functional elegance.

The following pages look at some of the major American residential styles and discuss why they are what they are and how they are recognized. Of course it is difficult to generalize about so complex a subject and the author has taken some liberties for the sake of brevity.

If there is a current style, it might be labeled "eclectic-modernism"— a move back toward the tenets of Modernism with a liberal use of Classical and borrowed form.

STYLE

<u>VICTORIAN</u>

The Victorian Style was born in the era
of Queen Victoria. It can be a mixture
of many styles but it especially borrows
from Gothic Revival. Technological advances
of the age such as the jig-saw are
reflected in the ornate wood detailing.

Ornate Chimney with
tall, slim proportions

Detailed Lattice woodwork

Tall, slim openings

Copious Verandas

Gingerbread wood
ornament, especially
diagonal bracing.

Lattice screen base

Multi-gabled roof

Steep gables
with diagonal
bracing

Assymetrical
Composition

Brickwork and
arches are a
holdover from
Romanesque
period - Exterior
may be wood
but forms are
similar.

STYLE

The Classical Revival style was a renaissance of Greek and Roman forms that swept the nation in the mid-nineteenth century. It was rich in symbol and ornament and used for every type of building which diluted the meaning.

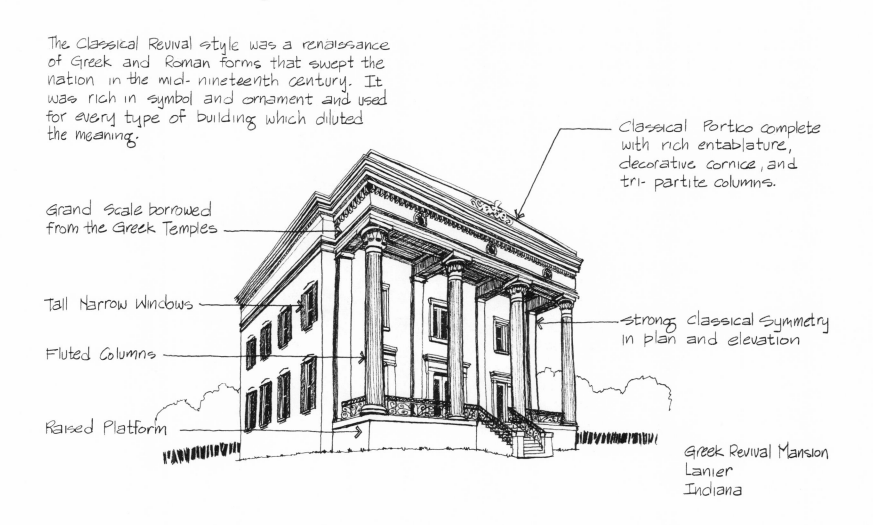

Classical Portico complete with rich entablature, decorative cornice, and tri-partite columns.

Grand Scale borrowed from the Greek Temples

Tall Narrow Windows

Fluted Columns

Raised Platform

strong classical symmetry in plan and elevation

Greek Revival Mansion
Lanier
Indiana

STYLE

COLONIAL

The Colonial Style was one of the earliest house styles in America. It continues to be popular because of its very efficient ratio of materials to space enclosed and its stately appearance.

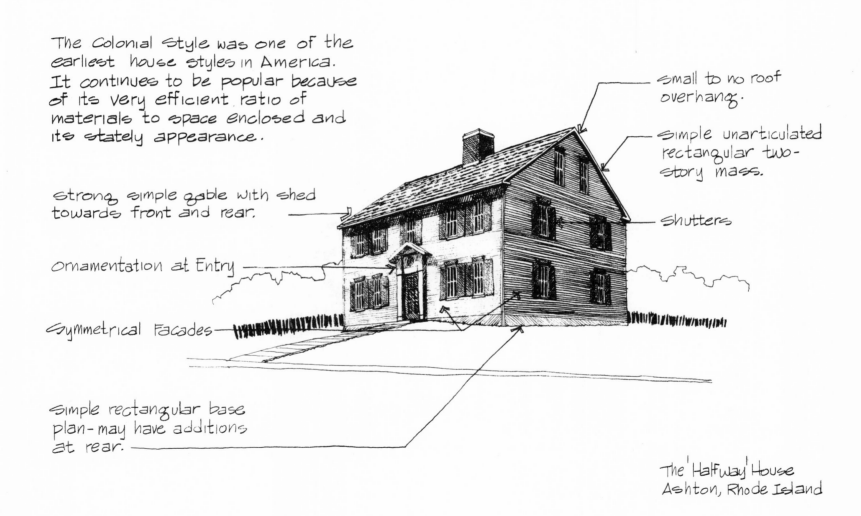

small to no roof overhang.

simple unarticulated rectangular two-story mass.

Shutters

Strong, simple gable with shed towards front and rear.

Ornamentation at Entry

Symmetrical Facades

Simple rectangular base plan-may have additions at rear.

The 'Halfway' House
Ashton, Rhode Island

The 'Bungalow' style came to the U.S. via the English presence in India where the Bengali house was a low structure with porches all around.

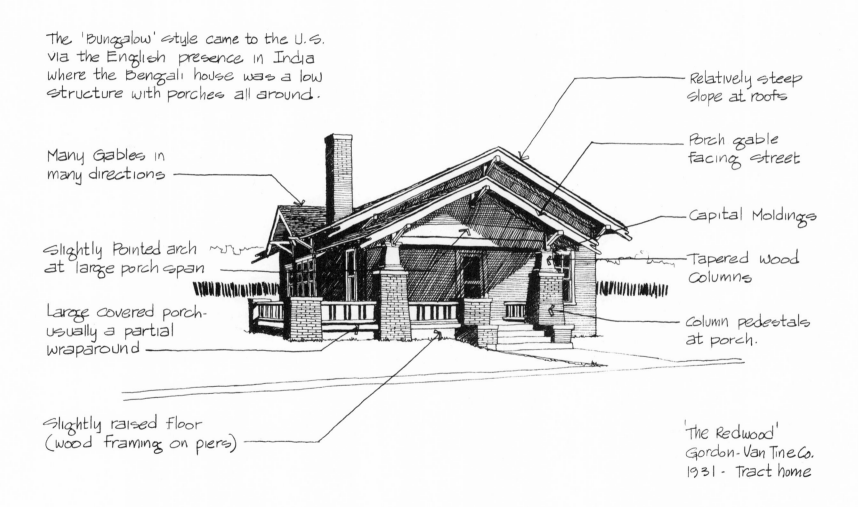

Many Gables in many directions

Relatively steep slope at roofs

Porch gable facing street

Capital Moldings

Slightly Pointed arch at large porch span

Tapered Wood Columns

Large Covered porch- usually a partial wraparound

Column pedestals at porch.

Slightly raised floor (wood framing on piers)

'The Redwood' Gordon-Van Tine Co. 1931 - Tract home

STYLE

PRAIRIE

The Prairie Style was the forerunner of the
Usonian House, predecessor to the popular
suburban 'Ranch Style' House.

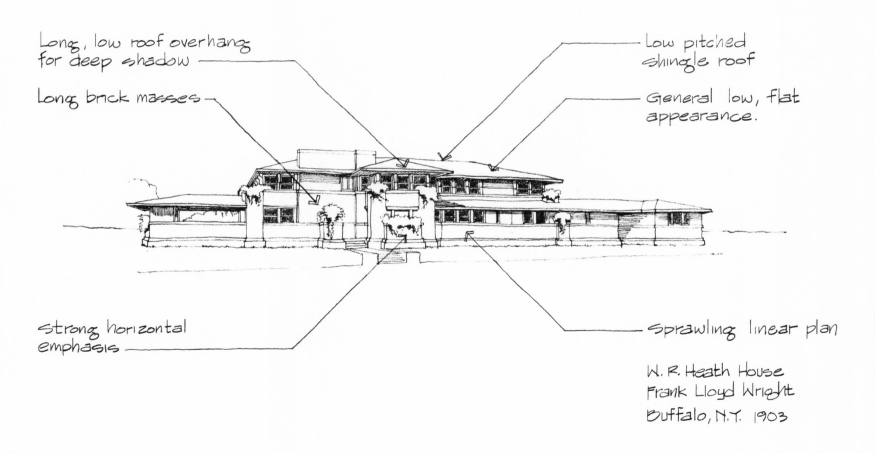

Long, low roof overhang
for deep shadow

Long brick masses

Low pitched
shingle roof

General low, flat
appearance.

strong horizontal
emphasis

Sprawling linear plan

W. R. Heath House
Frank Lloyd Wright
Buffalo, N.Y. 1903

The International Style was based not on any cultural evolution but on the honest expression of modern structural materials and principles of health, light, and air common throughout the world. Non-essential ornamentation was abandoned in favor of purity of form and abstract geometry. Functionalism was the key to the style.

Ribbon Windows

Exterior Wall expressed as a thin curtain

strong expression of structure

Columns expressed as plain shafts without base and capital.

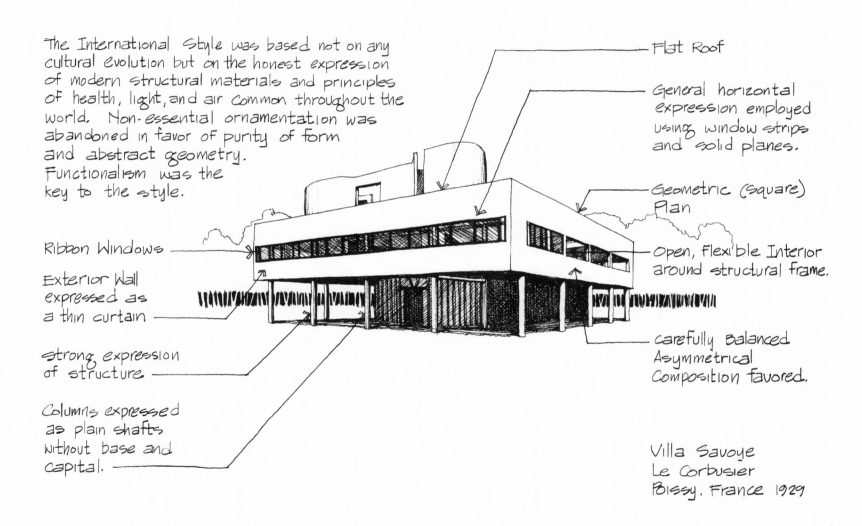

Flat Roof

General horizontal expression employed using window strips and solid planes.

Geometric (Square) Plan

Open, Flexible Interior around structural frame.

Carefully Balanced Asymmetrical Composition favored.

Villa Savoye
Le Corbusier
Poissy, France 1929

STYLE

MODERN

The Modern Style can be thought of as the most popular extension of the tenets of the International Style. It is concerned more with visual interest than a strict adherence to simplicity and purity of form.

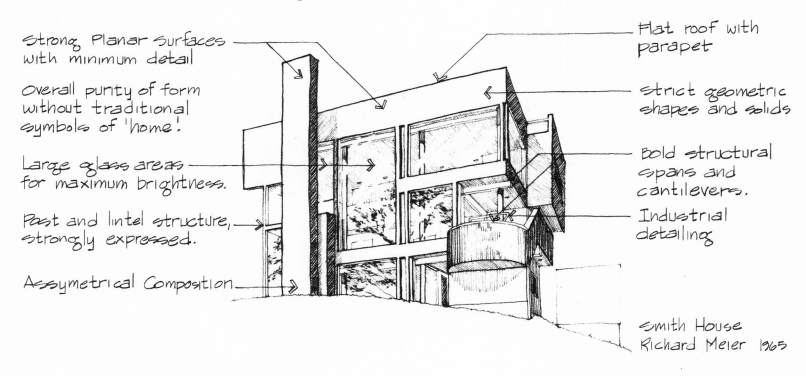

Strong Planar Surfaces with minimum detail

Overall purity of form without traditional symbols of 'home'.

Large glass areas for maximum brightness.

Post and lintel structure, strongly expressed.

Assymetrical Composition

Flat roof with parapet

Strict geometric shapes and solids

Bold structural spans and cantilevers.

Industrial detailing

Smith House
Richard Meier 1965

The Industrial Style is an extension
of the Modern with a strong emphasis
on prefabricated component parts
as building materials.

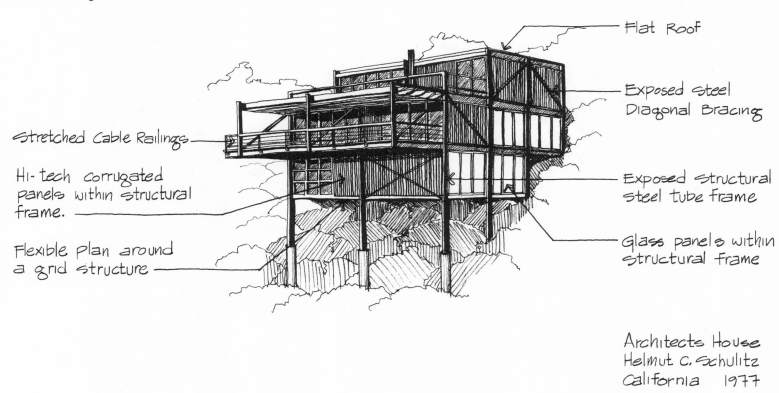

Flat Roof

Exposed Steel
Diagonal Bracing

Stretched Cable Railings

Hi-tech corrugated
panels within structural
frame.

Flexible plan around
a grid structure

Exposed structural
steel tube frame

Glass panels within
structural Frame

Architects House
Helmut C. Schulitz
California 1977

STYLE

POSTMODERN

As modern architecture became more abstract in its striving toward simplicity and consistency it removed itself more and more from public understanding and sympathy. Postmodernism represents a movement back toward a more humanistic architecture through purposeful complexity and the revival of historic forms and details.

Arches and other references to historic styles

Rearrangement of design elements to create new associations

Liberal use of moldings and other types of surface ornamentation.

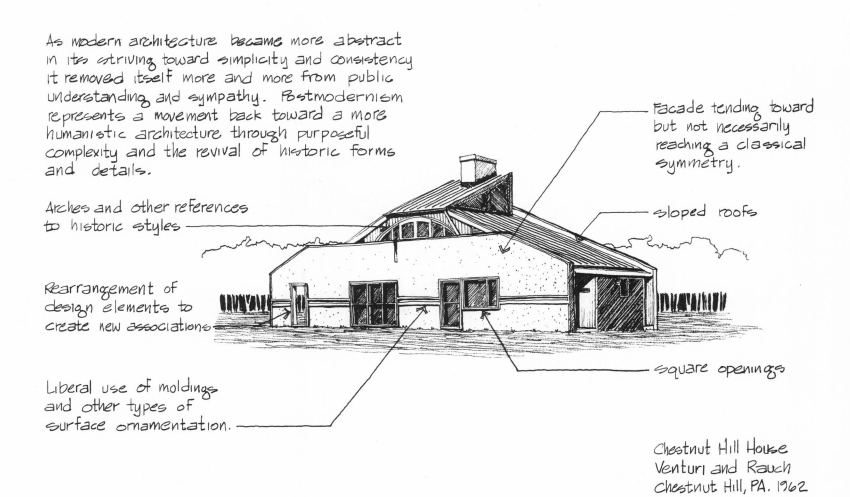

Facade tending toward but not necessarily reaching a classical symmetry.

sloped roofs

square openings

Chestnut Hill House
Venturi and Rauch
Chestnut Hill, PA. 1962

An organic style of architecture has always been a part of man's imagination.
It is not well-suited to accomodate the trappings of a rectangular world but the natural forms have a basic appeal.

Sculptural massing of curves without straight lines or right angles.

Operable windows are difficult with this style.

Shingles or sprayed gunite skin help to mold a watertight skin.

Irregular free-form plan

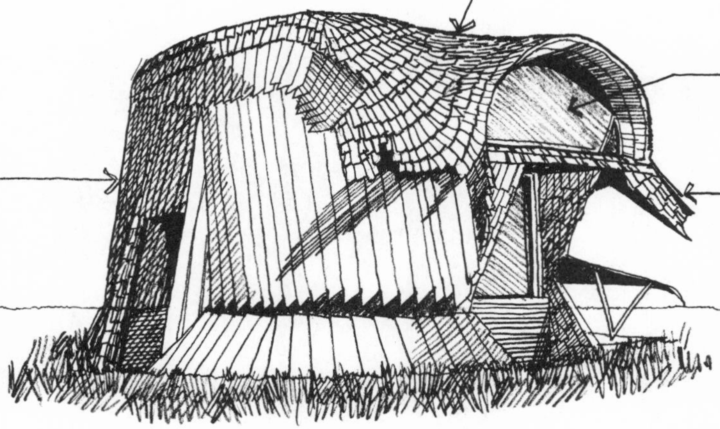

This house cannot be completely drawn so owner must actively participate in the construction process.

Architects House
Herb Greene
Norman, Ok.   1960

193

STYLE

Attempts to combine too many different
materials and styles may become awkward.

DETAILS

"God is in the detail".
　　　　Ludwig Mies Van Der Rohe

If we have made all the proper decisions up to this point, we have designed a superior house. The attention we give now to detail will make it a home. This level of design may be more subtle but this is the level we live on in our daily lives, the refinements that make the design truly personal.

This chapter contains some ideas which can be worked into any house design, making it more functional and/or pleasurable. Most are very inexpensive suggestions and many can be implemented by the owner after construction on the house is finished.

DETITAILS

There are two basic options for successful interior artificial lighting: Indirect and Incandescent. Indirect lighting means the observer cannot directly see the light source, which tends to be extremely bright in contrast to the light level of the room. The indirectness allows for a more subtle and even lighting situation and can produce a wide variety of moods.

Incandescent lighting refers to filament type bulbs, which emit light in the warmer yellow ranges rather than the cold bluer tones of most fluorescent bulbs. Incandescent bulbs can also be used with a dimmer switch more easily than fluorescent which guarantees exactly the right amount of light for each different task or mood.

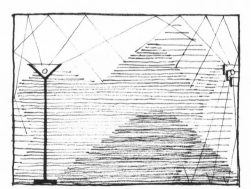

Ceiling lamps or wall-mounted sconces provide good quality indirect incandescent light.

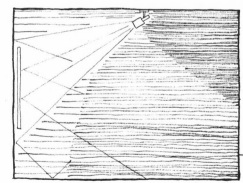

A ceiling mounted swivel spot-light in a box or on a track can provide dramatic indirect light when focused on artwork or a wall.

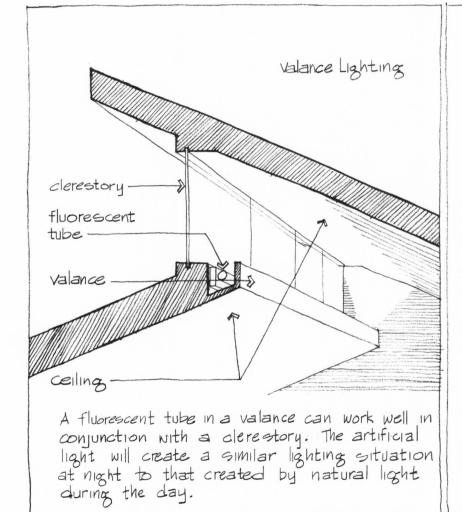

Valance Lighting

clerestory

fluorescent
tube

valance

ceiling

A fluorescent tube in a valance can work well in
conjunction with a clerestory. The artificial
light will create a similar lighting situation
at night to that created by natural light
during the day.

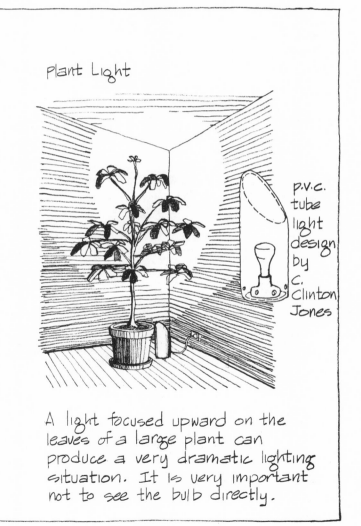

Plant Light

p.v.c.
tube
light
design
by
C.
Clinton
Jones

A light focused upward on the
leaves of a large plant can
produce a very dramatic lighting
situation. It is very important
not to see the bulb directly.

DETAILS

WINDOWS and VIEWS

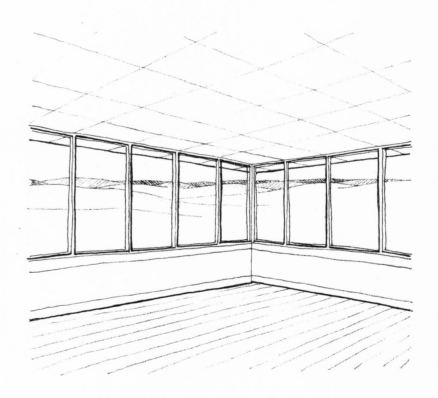

Bay windows offer a vantage point with a 180° view plus more glass area for the amount of wall space. The plan configuration penetrates the exterior and adds a focus to the space.

Corner windows and long glass bands can expand a space by bringing the outside in and extending the inside outward. This play between inside and out is an important element found in many great houses.

Window seats make very secure and comfortable reading niches, especially in winter.

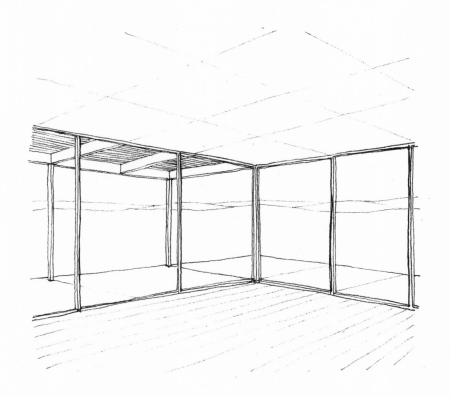

Interior space can be vastly increased psychologically by continuing the enclosure planes outside the enclosure.

DETAILS

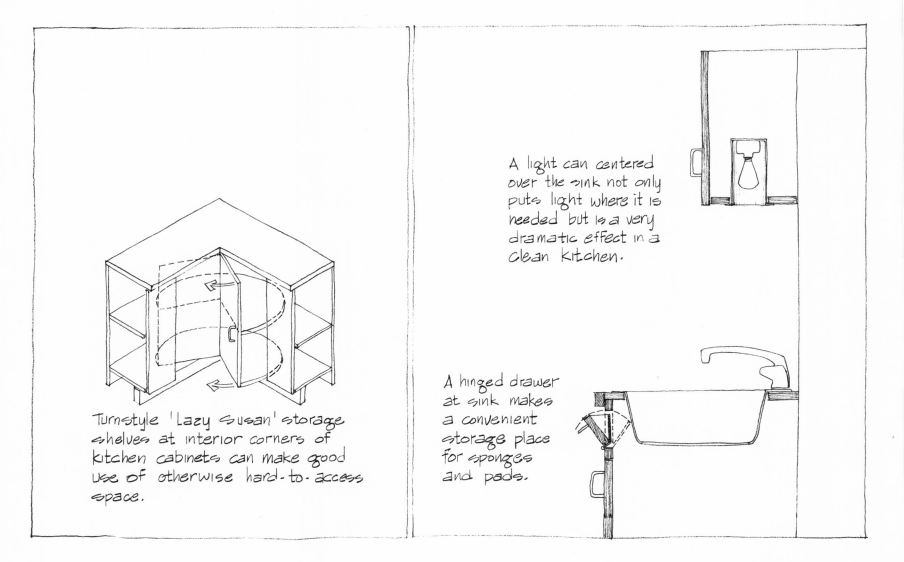

Turnstyle 'Lazy Susan' storage shelves at interior corners of kitchen cabinets can make good use of otherwise hard-to-access space.

A light can centered over the sink not only puts light where it is needed but is a very dramatic effect in a clean kitchen.

A hinged drawer at sink makes a convenient storage place for sponges and pads.

Plan view of Kitchen Pantry Storage Showing Operation

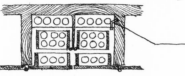

— 1x4 fixed shelves at rear

Closed Position

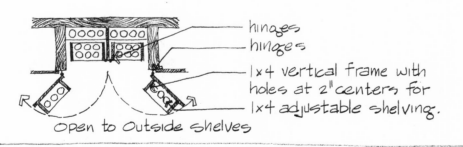

hinges
hinges

1x4 vertical frame with holes at 2" centers for

1x4 adjustable shelving.

Open to Outside Shelves

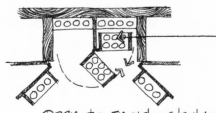

— 1x8 vertical frame with holes at 2" centers for 1x8 adjustable shelving.

Open to Inside Shelves

Canned food storage can be greatly increased as well as easily accessed with this design for layered storage shelves on hinges by Alfonso Varella.

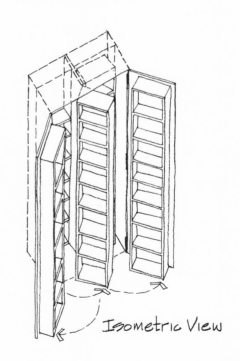

Isometric View

DETAILS

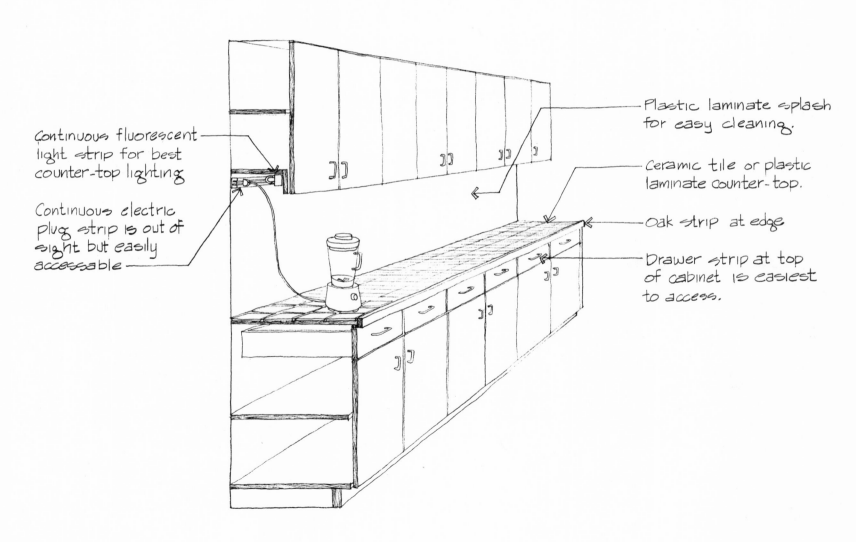

Continuous fluorescent light strip for best counter-top lighting

Continuous electric plug strip is out of sight but easily accessable

Plastic laminate splash for easy cleaning.

Ceramic tile or plastic laminate counter-top.

Oak strip at edge

Drawer strip at top of cabinet is easiest to access.

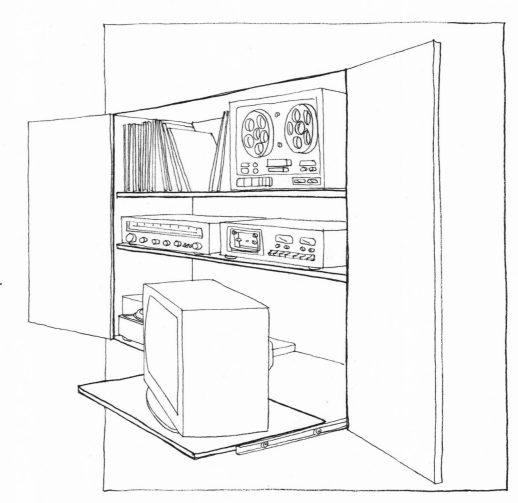

stereo equipment can be located
in a built-in electronics cabinet,
out of sight and easily locked-up.

Television on a swivel base
mounted on a sliding track
can be out of sight when
not in use.

DETAILS

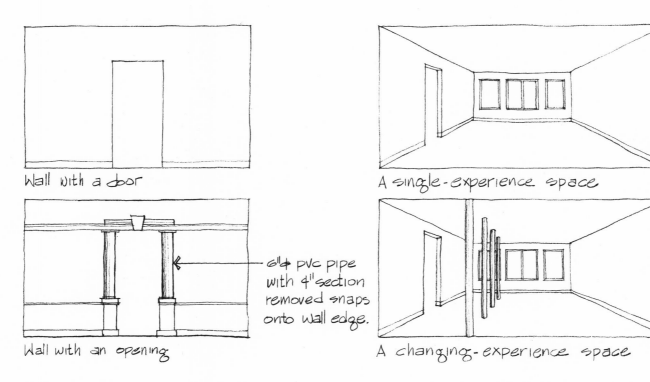

Wall with a door

A single-experience space

Wall with an opening

6"⌀ pvc pipe
with 4" section
removed snaps
onto wall edge.

A changing-experience space

With a little imagination and plywood,
a corridor entrance can become a
design element.

Columns in the right place can create a real
experience of space through movement,
by framing views and implicit transparent
planes. They can also be useful as implicit
space dividers and proportioners. 6" or 8"
round p.v.c. is inexpensive and perfect for this use.

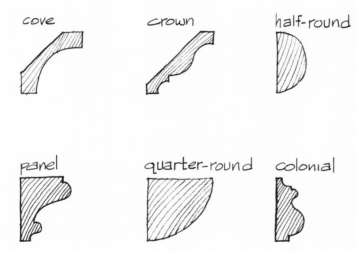

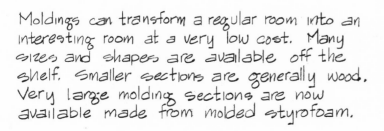

Moldings can transform a regular room into an interesting room at a very low cost. Many sizes and shapes are available off the shelf. Smaller sections are generally wood. Very large molding sections are now available made from molded styrofoam.

This material is soft but once painted, it looks and feels like plaster. Chair rails can also become a strong design element. A standard piece of 1x6 used as a base can have a much nicer effect than the more ordinary "sanitary trim" commonly used for this purpose.

DETAILS

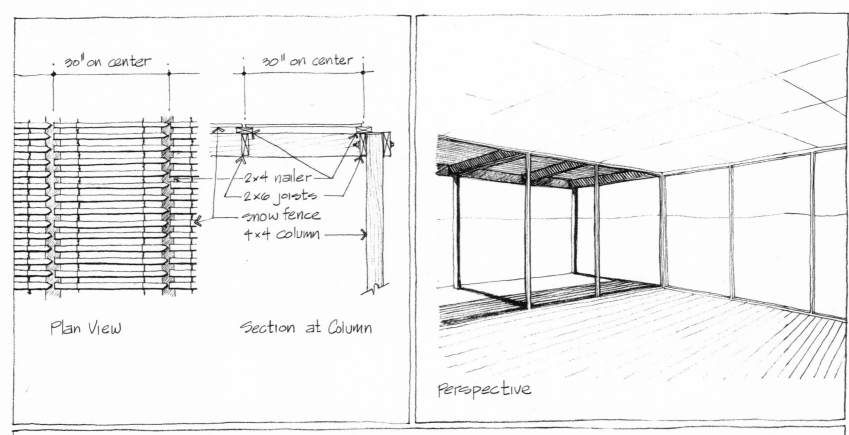

. 30" on center .

30" on center

2x4 nailer
2x6 joists
snow fence
4x4 Column

Plan View

Section at Column

Perspective

A wood trellis can extend a space out-of-doors as well as provide shade for large glass areas. This effect can be had at a very reasonable cost by using snow fencing over a 2x wood

frame instead of using expensive wood sticks. Clear plastic sheeting can be stapled on top of the trellis for a dry outdoor area if desired.

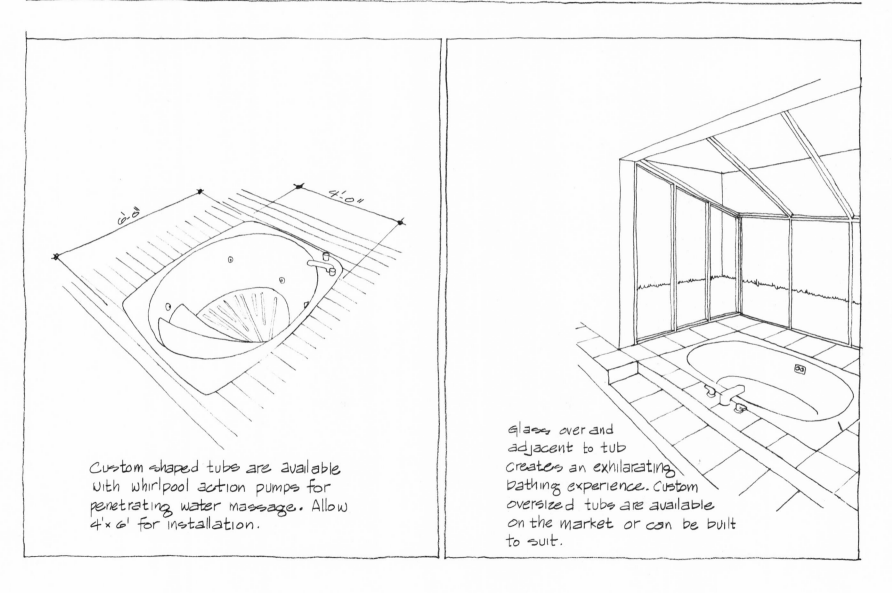

Custom shaped tubs are available with whirlpool action pumps for penetrating water massage. Allow 4'x 6' for installation.

Glass over and adjacent to tub creates an exhilarating bathing experience. Custom oversized tubs are available on the market or can be built to suit.

DETAILS

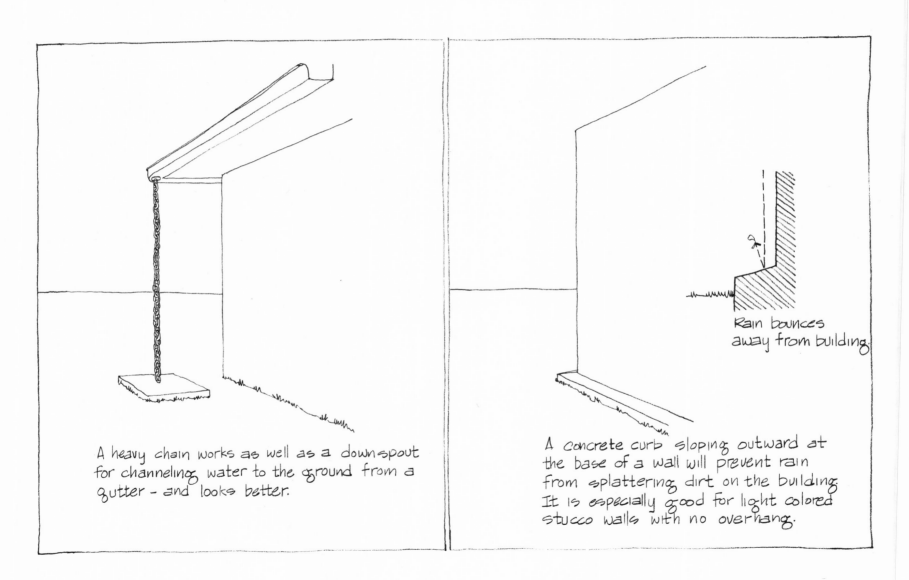

A heavy chain works as well as a downspout for channeling water to the ground from a gutter - and looks better.

Rain bounces away from building.

A concrete curb sloping outward at the base of a wall will prevent rain from splattering dirt on the building. It is especially good for light colored stucco walls with no overhang.

208

APPENDIX

INTRODUCTION

There are many methods and machines made to conserve energy and utilize the natural resources of the environment. Most of these have become very complex propositions as the theories have been refined, however the basic principles are relatively simple. This chapter gives a brief overview of some of the more popular types and descriptions of how they work. Most will present a cost premium in times of low energy prices but these times are not always with us. Many solar techniques are not efficient in every climate. The following pages should help you to decide if more investigation is worthwhile.

APPENDIX

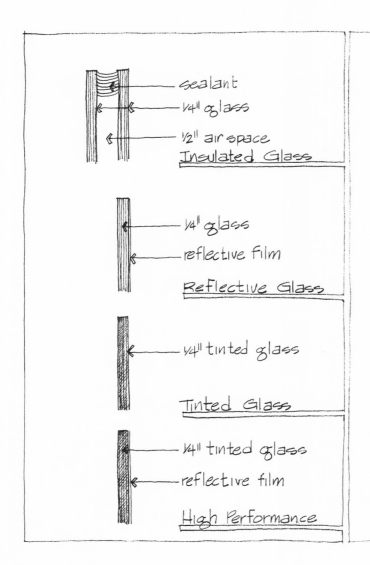

sealant
¼" glass
½" air space
Insulated Glass

¼" glass
reflective film
Reflective Glass

¼" tinted glass
Tinted Glass

¼" tinted glass
reflective film
High Performance

Insulated glass is a term for double-glazed windows which have a high resistance to conductive heat transfer. Two layers of glass with an air space between can cut the overall coefficient of heat transmission (U-value) in half. This glass is expensive but can be amortized quickly in the colder climates.

Reflective glass means glass with a reflective coating applied to the inside surface. This coating reduces the transfer of heat through radiation by reflecting direct sunlight back to the outdoors. The extra price is quickly amortized in sunny areas but this glass has a solid, mirror aesthetic that is objectionable to many people, especially in residential uses.

Tinted glass will also reduce radiation heat gain although not nearly as effectively as reflective glass. Tinted glass comes in gray, bronze, green or blue tints

High Performance Glass is a term applied to tinted-reflective glass which is very effective at reducing radiation heat gain. The tint also reduces the mirror-like appearance to a very acceptable level.

Insulation is a material that impedes the flow of heat. There are two basic types prevalent in the residential market, fiberglass batts and foam board. A fiberglass batt is a loosely woven blanket of fiberglass affixed to a plastic film, usually 4" thick. Foam board is usually a rigid styrofoam material. One inch of foam board has approximately the same heat flow resistance as 4" of fiberglass but it is more expensive.

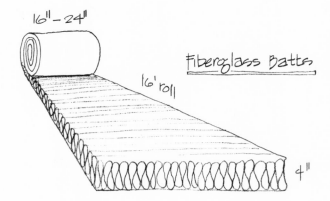

16" – 24"

16' roll

Fiberglass Batts

4"

4'-0"

Foam Board

8'-0"

1"

Super-Insulation is a term used by home builders to attract an energy conscious public. It usually refers to wall construction of 6" studs and 6" fiberglass batt insulation. It is very effective at restricting heat flow through the wall. However, heat still flows very well through glass and an average house may lose 85-90% of its total heat loss through windows and doors. One should consider very carefully the extra expense of 6" stud construction when determining the cost effectiveness of super-insulation.

APPENDIX

SOLAR WATER HEATER

A typical solar collector is a metal tray painted black with a metal tube attached to it or embedded within it. Water enters the tube at the bottom, is heated, and leaves at the top. There are many manufactured systems on the market that work extremely well.

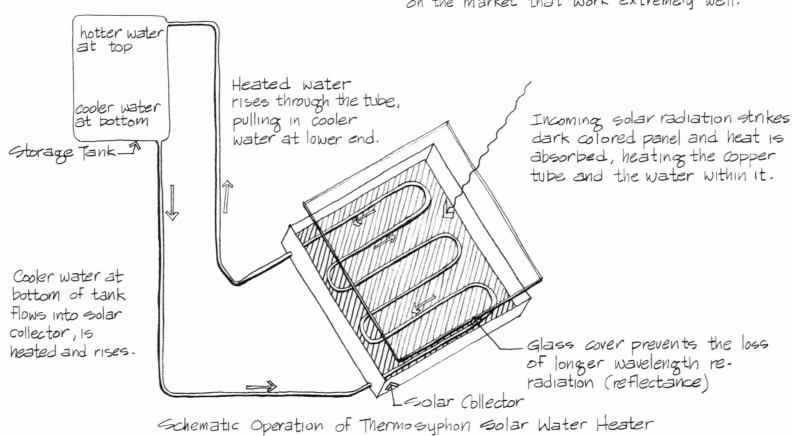

hotter water at top

cooler water at bottom

Storage Tank

Heated water rises through the tube, pulling in cooler water at lower end.

Incoming solar radiation strikes dark colored panel and heat is absorbed, heating the copper tube and the water within it.

Cooler water at bottom of tank flows into solar collector, is heated and rises.

Glass cover prevents the loss of longer wavelength re-radiation (reflectance)

Solar Collector

Schematic Operation of Thermosyphon Solar Water Heater

ROOF PONDING

This passive solar system is especially useful in climates with hot days and cool nights. It is composed of water storage tanks mounted on a roof or in a south wall, behind an operable insulated cover.

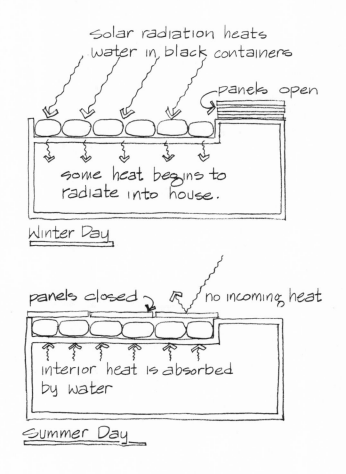

Solar radiation heats water in black containers

panels open

some heat begins to radiate into house.

Winter Day

panels closed

no incoming heat

interior heat is absorbed by water

Summer Day

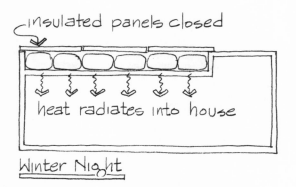

insulated panels closed

heat radiates into house

Winter Night

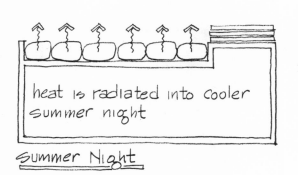

heat is radiated into cooler summer night

Summer Night

APPENDIX

The solar envelope house has been shown to be a very effective passive solar concept with remarkable energy efficiency.

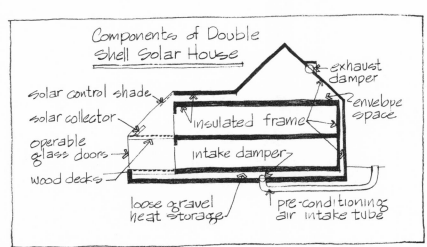

Components of Double Shell Solar House

- solar control shade
- solar collector
- operable glass doors
- wood decks
- insulated frame
- intake damper
- exhaust damper
- envelope space
- loose gravel heat storage
- pre-conditioning air intake tube

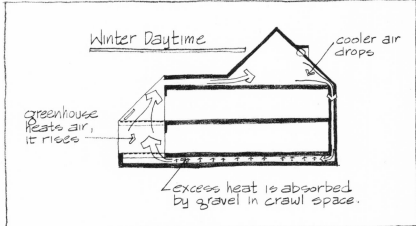

Winter Daytime

- cooler air drops
- greenhouse heats air, it rises
- excess heat is absorbed by gravel in crawl space.

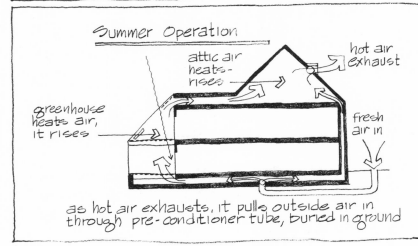

Summer Operation

- attic air heats-rises
- hot air exhaust
- greenhouse heats air, it rises
- fresh air in

as hot air exhausts, it pulls outside air in through pre-conditioner tube, buried in ground

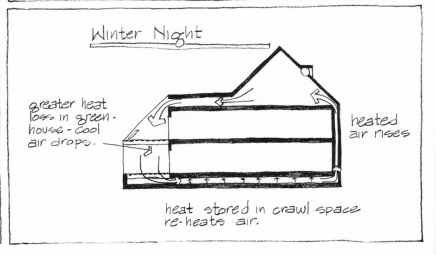

Winter Night

- greater heat loss in green-house - cool air drops.
- heated air rises

heat stored in crawl space re-heats air.

EARTH BERM HOUSE

The energy consumption of a heating or cooling system is directly related to the difference between the outside and inside temperatures. This is the principle of the earth berm house. The earth is a relatively constant 65° all year round, not far from the comfort range of humans which is between 72°- 75°F. The idea is to surround as much of the house perimeter as possibe with earth, reducing the heat loss or gain considerably through those walls.

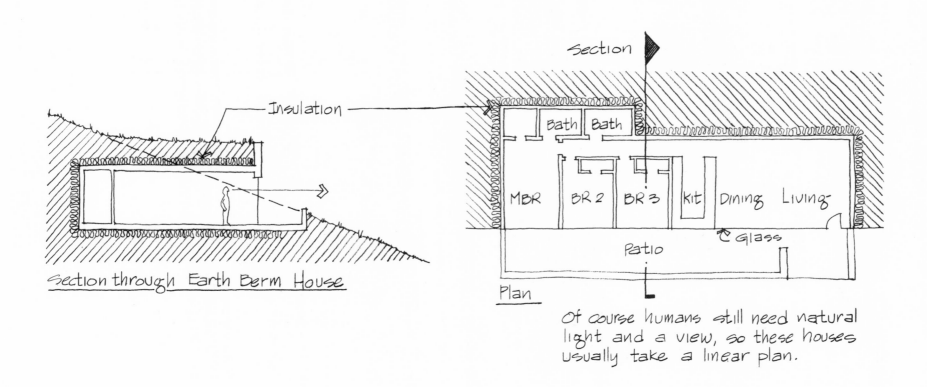

Section through Earth Berm House

Of course humans still need natural light and a view, so these houses usually take a linear plan.

APPENDIX

THERMAL LAG

Thermal lag is a concept based on the time required for heat to travel through massive, dense materials such as stone or brick. This concept is valid only for hot day - cool night climates such as Colorado since it is based on a 24 hour cool / hot cycle.

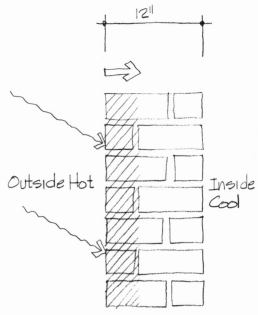

Daytime - solar radiation heats exterior surface, heat begins to move through wall.

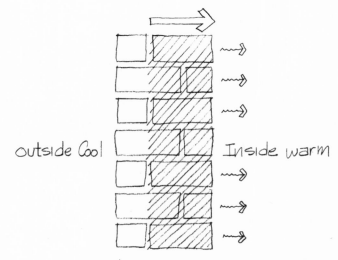

Night - Heat has passed through wall and begins to warm house interior. Cool night begins to lower temperature of exterior wall surface.

A Trombe Wall is a massive dark-colored masonry wall placed behind glass acting as a passive solar collector. It is usually concrete block or brick, built in two wythes (layers) with an air space (6") between for air flow.

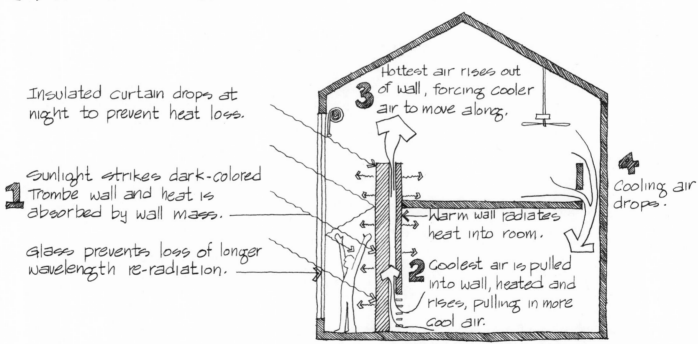

Insulated curtain drops at night to prevent heat loss.

3 Hottest air rises out of wall, forcing cooler air to move along.

1 Sunlight strikes dark-colored Trombe wall and heat is absorbed by wall mass.

Glass prevents loss of longer wavelength re-radiation.

Warm wall radiates heat into room.

4 Cooling air drops.

2 Coolest air is pulled into wall, heated and rises, pulling in more cool air.

For best results, the glass wall should be insulated at night to prevent heat loss through that vulnerable part of the system.

Retractable insulated curtains are manufactured for that purpose, or a home-made system of styrofoam panels will do the trick.

APPENDIX

HEAT PUMPS

The basic principle of any air conditioner is to transfer heat from one area to another. Most air conditioning systems remove heat from the inside and deposit it outside using a cycle of compressing and expanding refrigerant gases such as freon.

A heat pump employs this same cycle except it can be switched to reverse the cycle and thereby remove heat from the outside and deposit it inside during winter.

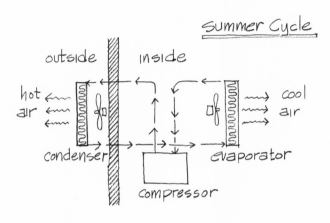

Summer Cycle

outside   inside

hot air ←   cool air →
condenser   evaporator
compressor

In the summer cycle, the heat pump is as efficient as any standard air conditioner. In the winter cycle, it is more efficient than other types of electric heating at outside temperatures above 40°F. Below 40°F, the efficiency falls off rapidly and supplemental sources of heat may be required.

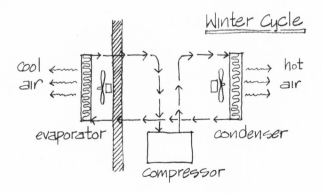

Winter Cycle

cool air ←   hot air →
evaporator   condenser
compressor

WATER HEAT EXCHANGER

The efficiency (operating cost) of any air conditioning system is directly related to the efficiency of heat exchange that takes place at the condenser. Most residential units have an air-to-air exchange, i.e., heat removed from the system by a fan moving air across the coils.

Water has a specific heat value almost twice that of air which means it is almost twice as efficient at heat removal.

This system is especially good with heat pumps since the water would usually be well above the 40°F break point of the heat pump. A great deal can be saved on operating costs. The water, however, must be filtered and pumped through the condenser which will add a maintenance factor as well as some front-end costs.

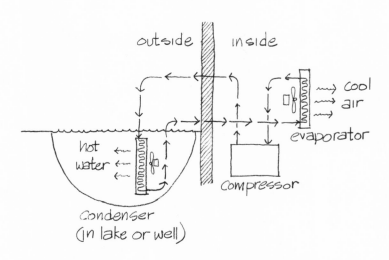

Operational Schematic of Air Conditioning System Using a Water Heat Exchanger

APPENDIX

FIREPLACE DESIGN

A standard fireplace is comforting to behold; however, it may be the greatest source of heat loss in the house. While you feel the warmth of the radiated heat, your chimney draft may be pulling all the heated air outside the house faster than you can heat it up. There are a few details which can increase the efficiency of a fireplace considerably:

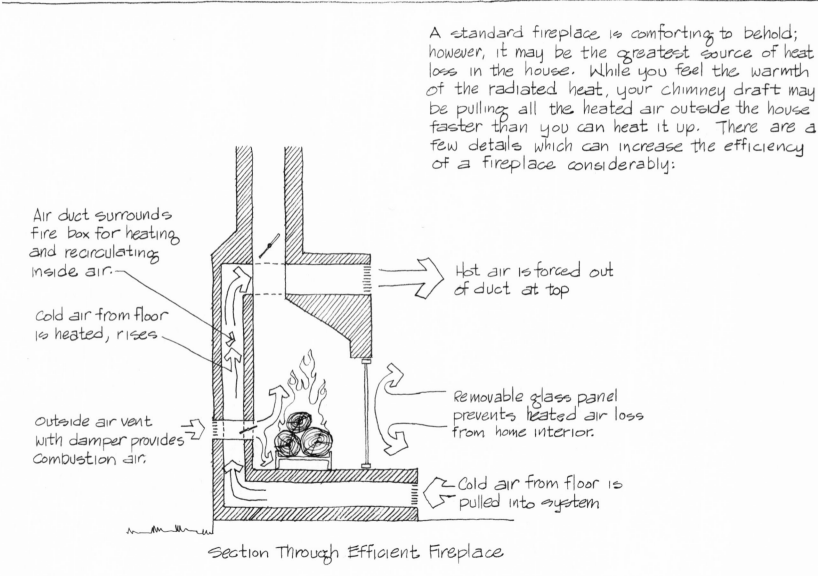

Air duct surrounds fire box for heating and recirculating inside air.

Cold air from floor is heated, rises

Outside air vent with damper provides combustion air.

Hot air is forced out of duct at top

Removable glass panel prevents heated air loss from home interior.

Cold air from floor is pulled into system

Section Through Efficient Fireplace

Natural ventilation principles can be applied to any house design. They work especially well in areas with longer temperate seasons and low humidity.

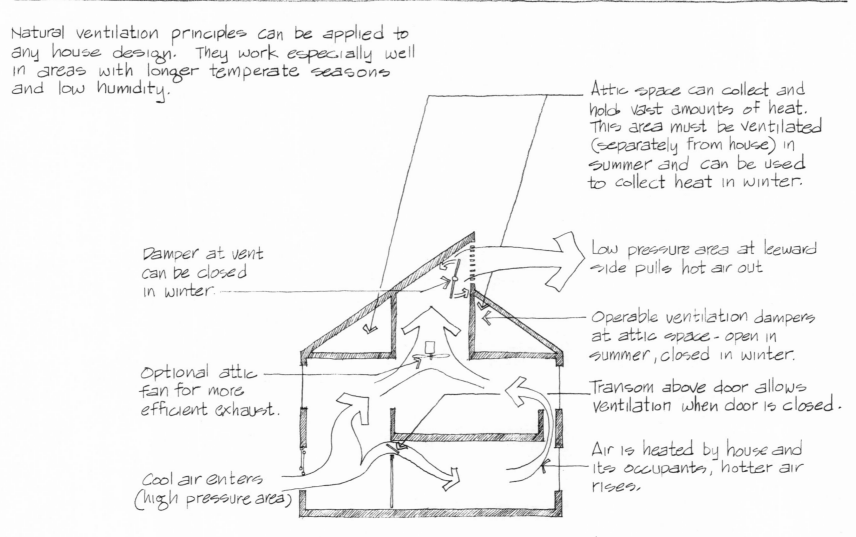

Attic space can collect and hold vast amounts of heat. This area must be ventilated (separately from house) in summer and can be used to collect heat in winter.

Damper at vent can be closed in winter.

Low pressure area at leeward side pulls hot air out

Operable ventilation dampers at attic space - open in summer, closed in winter.

Optional attic fan for more efficient exhaust.

Transom above door allows ventilation when door is closed.

Cool air enters (high pressure area)

Air is heated by house and its occupants, hotter air rises.

Section thru Naturally Ventilated House

APPENDIX

<u>COLD CLIMATE DESIGN</u>

Cold climates may not require air conditioning in summer months if house is designed for natural ventilation. Refer to appendix section on ventilation for concepts.

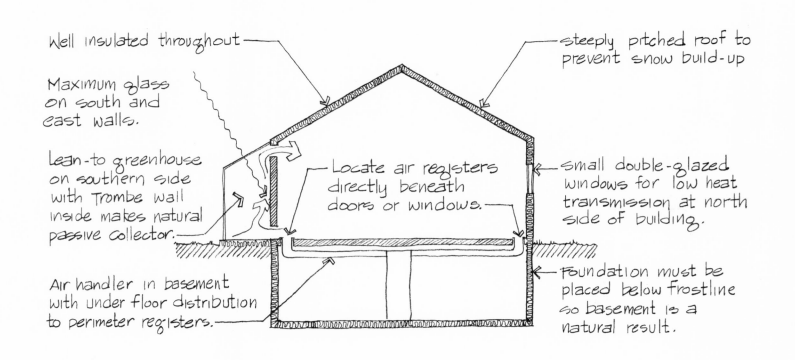

Well insulated throughout

Maximum glass on south and east walls.

Lean-to greenhouse on southern side with Trombe wall inside makes natural passive collector.

Air handler in basement with under floor distribution to perimeter registers.

Locate air registers directly beneath doors or windows.

steeply pitched roof to prevent snow build-up

small double-glazed windows for low heat transmission at north side of building.

Foundation must be placed below frostline so basement is a natural result.

HOT DAYS - COOL NIGHTS CLIMATE

Thermal lag and solar concepts work very well in these climates. Collectors can gain and store heat during winter days for night use. Storage tank can gain heat from house during summer days and radiate it to cool summer nights.

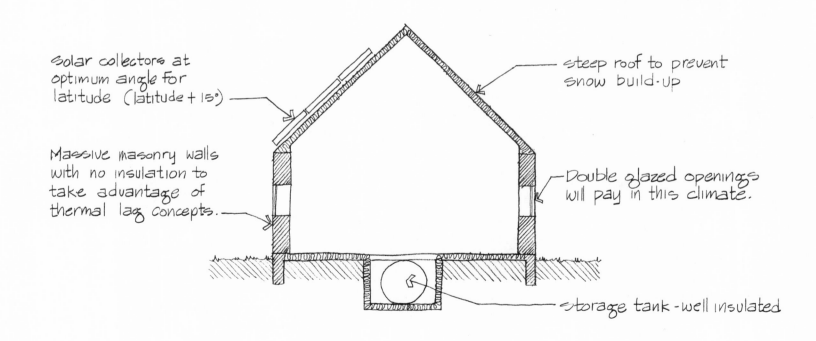

Solar collectors at optimum angle for latitude (latitude + 15°)

Massive masonry walls with no insulation to take advantage of thermal lag concepts.

steep roof to prevent snow build-up

Double glazed openings will pay in this climate.

storage tank - well insulated

APPENDIX

Hot Day and night climates are usually very humid and require a good air conditioning system to reduce both temperature and humidity. Heat pumps are ideal for these climates since winters are usually not severe. Solar or thermal lag systems are not very effective because of the hot nights.

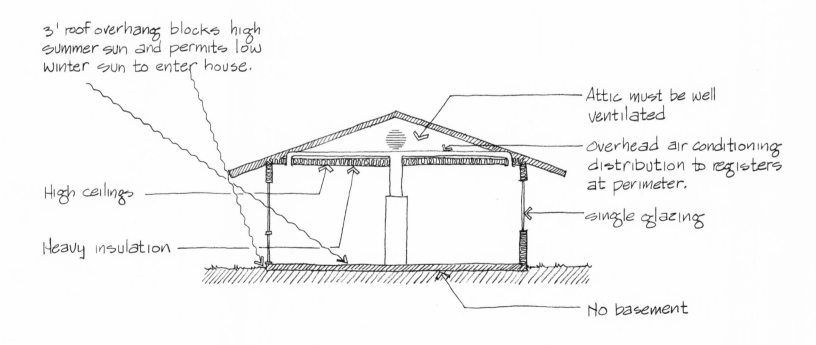

3' roof overhang blocks high summer sun and permits low winter sun to enter house.

High ceilings

Heavy insulation

Attic must be well ventilated

Overhead air conditioning distribution to registers at perimeter.

single glazing

No basement

GLOSSARY

GLOSSARY

Materials Symbols

	Earth
	Loose Fill
	Concrete
	Metal
	Masonry
	Finish Wood

	Rough Wood
	Batt Insulation
	Rigid Insulation

Plan Symbols

	Standard Door
	Bi-fold Door
	Flexible Partition

	Sliding Glass Door
	Window

Electrical Symbols

	Ceiling Light Fixture
	Wall Light Fixture
	220-240 volt outlet
	110-120 volt outlet

⊙	Floor Outlet
Ⓣ	Thermostat
Wall switch symbol	Wall Switch
3-way switch symbol	3-way Wall Switch
Special outlet symbol	Special outlet w/ note for TV, stereo, etc
Supply duct symbol	Supply Duct Ceiling Diffuser
Return air duct symbol	Return air Duct or Exhaust

Fan symbol	Fan

Equipment Symbols

Sink symbol	Kitchen Sinks with Disposal
Dishwasher symbol	Undercounter Dishwasher
Trash compacter symbol	Undercounter Trash Compacter
Cabinet doors symbol	Cabinet Doors w/ hinges at outside
Lavatory symbol	Bathroom Lavoratory

Freestanding lavatory symbol	Free standing Lavoratory
Watercloset symbol	Watercloset
Shower symbol	Shower
Bathtub symbol	Bathtub
W. D.	Washer-Dryer
HWH	Hot Water Heater
Spiral stair symbol UP	Spiral Stair

227

GLOSSARY

TERMS

Arch- Structure spanning an opening with small wedge shape members placed perpendicular to the curve.

Architrave - The lower portion of an entablature above the column, or the molded frame around an opening. See Classical Order.

Awning - A rooflike cover extending over an opening.

Axial - Linear organization of elements, usually an axis between two points.

Band Window - Windows set one directly adjacent to another with little or no separation.

Base - The lower portion in the Classical Tripartite Order. Also, the trim at the joint of the floor and wall.

Beam - Major horizontal structural element supporting secondary structural members.

Berm - Sculptured earth mound used in conjunction with landscape design.

Brace - Stabilizing element in a structural frame, usually a diagonal member.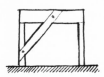

Bridging - Bracing for secondary structural members which helps load sharing by the adjacent members.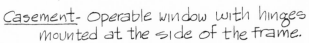

Cantilever - A beam supported at one end, projecting from the support.

Canopy - A lightweight roof membrane usually canvas stretched over a metal frame.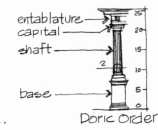

Capital - The top portion of the Classical Tripartite Order.

Casement - Operable window with hinges mounted at the side of the frame.

Classical Order - A set of proportions found in antiquity, which regulate the dimensions of base, shaft, capital, entablature, spacing, etc., based on the diameter of the shaft.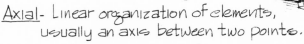

entablature
capital
shaft
2
base

Doric Order

Clapboard - Wood siding with one thin edge to lap over the member below.

GLOSSARY

Column - The vertical structural element in a frame, supporting beams.

Composition - The arrangement of elements in an orderly, pleasing manner.

Control Joint - Thin linear space between large areas of material which allows for temperature expansion and contraction, and controls the location of cracking.

Corbel - Projecting elements from a wall such as bricks, usually decorative in nature.

Cornice - The projecting element at the top of the entablature.

Dormer - Roof structure accomodating a vertical window set in a sloping roof.

Double Hung - Window divided horizontally in which top and bottom sections are both operable, sliding up and down.

Dry-Vit - A brand name connoting a stucco-like material applied over styrofoam board.

Duct - A tube which channels air flow from the blower in a central air conditioning system.

Easement - Right of use of a portion of one person's land by another person or authority.

Entablature - That portion of the structure above the column capital and below the roof or pediment in Classical Architure. See Classical Order.

Elevation - The face of a building, viewed straight-on, without perspective distortion.

Facade - The face or front of a building.

Fascia - A flat band along the edge of a roof or cornice.

Flashing - Sheet metal or membrane laid under roofing for water-proofing joints or seams.

flashing
built-up roof

Flute - Regularly spaced parallel grooves, usually on a column.

Footing - Thick concrete slab at the base of a foundation to dis-tribute structural loads to soil.

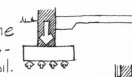

Furring - A covering finish material set out from the rough structure.

finish mat'l

Gable - Triangular wall segment at the end of a sloped roof.

GLOSSARY

TERMS

Gambrel - Roof shape with two slopes on each side, the lower being the steeper.

Girder - Primary horizontal members in a structural frame, sometimes supporting beams.

Glazing - Glass fitted into an opening.

Gunite - Cement and sand mixture applied with a spray nozzle onto a steel netting.

Hardware - Metal finish parts of a building such as door knobs, hinges, locksets, etc.

Head - The top horizontal section of an opening in a wall.

Hipped Roof - A roof type sloped on four sides.

Jamb - Vertical sections forming the sides of an opening.

Lantern - An open structure atop a roof allowing light into the space below.

Lean-to - A structural addition to the side of a building with a single sloped roof.

Mansard - A sloped wall made to look like a part of the roof, on four sides of the building, with windows.

Masonry - Constructed of materials laid by masons - brick, stone, concrete block, etc.

Molding - Thin trim materials with a decorative cross section used for concealing joints or decoration. Cyma recta

Mullion - The slender bar between the sections of glass in a window.

Parapet - A low wall at the edge of a flat roof or balcony.

Pediment - A triangular element in the classical style at the end facade of a gabled roof, over entrances or windows.

Pier and Beam - Foundation type consisting of a post set in the ground, supporting floor beams.

Plate - Horizontal member which carries wall studs, roof trusses or rafters.

Podium - A low foundation platform or base.

Portal - Main entrance into a building or city.

Port Coché - A large lightweight roof structure covering the vehicular entrance or drop-off.

Post and Lintel - Simple column and beam construction.

Press Board - Sheathing of reconstituted wood particles bonded together with epoxy.

Program - The written discription of functional requirements for spaces within a building.

Proportion - The relationship of one dimension to another - see scale.

$$\boxed{\frac{a}{b}=2} \; \frac{a}{} \; b$$

Rafter - Sloped secondary wood structural members in a roof frame.

Rebar - Steel reinforcing bar providing tensile strength in concrete.

Reveal - A purposeful joint used as a neutral space between two materials.

Running Bond - Traditional brick pattern with vertical joints offset by one-half the brick length.

Rustication - Massive masonry blocks separated by deep joints as in a rustic or rural manner.

Sash - The operable part of a window.

Scale - The relative proportion of a thing to a known size. thing→ brick→

Set-back - Specified distance from a property line to the point a building may begin.

Shaft - The central portion of the Classical Tripartite order.

Sheathing - Sheet material used to enclose a building

Sill - Horizontal element that forms the bottom of an opening.

Soffit - The underside of a roof overhang.

Spandrel - Opaque wall surface between windows.

Stringer - Sloped and notched structural member of a stair onto which the runners are fixed.

Stub-out - Exposed plumbing lines without fixtures.

Stucco - Cement and sand exterior plaster finish material applied with a trowel.

GLOSSARY

TERMS

<u>Studs</u> - Individual members of a wall to which the sheathing is attached.

<u>Tracery</u> - Perforated pattern of ornamental trim generally associated with openings, especially in the Victorian Era.

<u>Truss</u> - Structural member composed of light small pieces arranged to act as one deep element.

<u>Vault</u> - A masonry arch elongated to ceiling proportions.

<u>Visqueen</u> - Thin sheet of plastic used for waterproofing.

<u>Wainscot</u> - The lower section of an interior wall when finished in a different material from the wall.

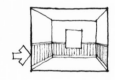

<u>Zone</u> - A term denoting area differtation in a plan for reasons of function, privacy, mechanical requirements, etc.

BIBLIOGRAPHY

Ching, Francis D.K. Architecture: Form, Space, & Order. New York: Van Nostrand Reinhold Co., 1979

Fletcher, Sir Banister. A History of Architecture. 18th Ed. Revised by J.C. Palmes. New York: Charles Scribner's Sons, 1975

Giedion, Siegfried. Space, Time, and Architecture. 4th Ed. Cambridge: Harvard University Press, 1968

Grillo, Paul Jacques. Form, Function, & Design. New York: Dover Publications, Inc., 1975

Le Corbusier. Towards A New Architecture. New York: Praeger Publishers, 1974.

McGuerty, Dave; Lester, Kent. The Complete Guide to Contracting Your Home. White Hall, Va. Betterway Publications, Inc. 1986

Moore, Charles; Allen, Gerald; Lyndon, Donlyn. The Place of Houses. New York: Holt, Reinhart and Winston, 1974.

Norberg-Schulz, Christian. Genius Loci. New York: Rizzoli, 1980.

Meaning in Western Architecture. New York: Praeger Publishers, 1975

Pevsner, Nikolaus. A History of Building Types. Princeton: Princeton University Press, 1976

Stern, Robert A.M. New Directions in American Architecture, New York: George Braziller, 1982

INDEX

---

556 306CLB 4060
BR
09/09